OLD LINE LINE PLATE

Readers' Collection

Kara Mae Harris

First Edition

Design by Kara Mae Harris
ISBN: 979-8-9882619-1-9

Published by Old Line Plate
www.oldlineplate.com

Dedicated to the kind and generous
Old Line Plate readers who have
helped me, through the solitary act
of writing, to make friends across
Maryland and the world.

Contents

Introduction

I am proud of the research that I do for Old Line Plate. I never tire of the cooking and the discovery. But I have to admit, no acknowledgement thrills me more than the fact that people are reading —and even enjoying—what I write.

I've wanted to be a writer since I was a child. To this day I continually take courses and read books to improve. I doubt I will ever feel that I've learned enough.

The fact that these recipes have brought me back around to something I love is not lost on me. With the Old Line Plate database and blog, I have managed to combine parts of myself and pursue my interests all while practicing the craft of writing good stories.

All this is to say that I present this book to those readers who don't have the time or patience to sit down with my larger hardcover books in hand. Here is the portable Old Line Plate: a collection of stories to bring with you on the bus or the breakroom, to read and dog-ear and pass on to friends.

I've included recipes not necessarily for cooking, but as part of the text for reference.

Who knows - this may be the first of many books. Even if it's not, I am satisfied with what I have accomplished. Young Kara would be sufficiently impressed.

I can't say that all of the writing within this book is my best work. I hope that's to come. But there are stories here that were worth telling. As long as that is the case and I am able, I will keep on writing.

Old Line Plate: An Overview

From "Old Line Plate: Stories & Recipes from Maryland"

Maryland food used to be famous across the Western World. Allegedly, one Baltimore caterer shipped his terrapin soup to London. Deviled crabs were popular wherever crabs could safely be shipped (and possibly where they couldn't). Canvasback duck was famous far and wide. Maryland Fried Chicken used to be a standard for luxury hotels and railroads - a version of it appeared on a menu for the Titanic. At the time, our beloved crabcakes were merely a footnote.

Not many people know what Maryland Fried Chicken is anymore, and it's nearly impossible to find Maryland beaten biscuits, let alone White Potato Pie. And (maybe thankfully) I haven't heard of anyone in my generation eating Maryland's famous diamondback terrapin.

When I started Old Line Plate, I had no idea that "Maryland Food" had a particularly notable history and distinction, let alone that it had ever had any kind of prestige. Sticking to Maryland recipes was merely a way to limit the scope of the project.

I had been collecting the Southern Heritage Cookbook Library that I'd known from my mother's kitchen. Inside the books, I found some recipes that surprised me: Southern Maryland Stuffed Ham, Maryland Fried Chicken, Maryland White Potato Pie.

I embarked on a quest to make some of these unfamiliar recipes. I thought I could simply follow each recipe line by line and taste history, like a culinary time machine.

It didn't quite go as planned, for many reasons.

A lot of old recipes are pretty vague. Standard measurements, consistent ovens - or even having an oven at all - couldn't be taken for granted until the 20th century. When some of these recipes were written, it was assumed that cooks would have a good amount of prior knowledge. Recipes for baked goods might list ingredients but then just say "cook in a slow oven."

Sometimes they wouldn't even remind you to cook it at all. I once made a doughnut recipe that ended with "wet it with milk into a light dough, and set to rise." Meat recipes; I sometimes wonder why they even bothered. A recipe for "English Meat Pie" called for "any kind of cold meat" with a "rich gravy or butter." For cooking raw meat they would just say "stew it until done."

Many of my oldest cookbooks are from the late 1800s. There was an explosion of cookbook publication in the 2nd half of the nineteenth century. The target audience were middle and upper-class white women; the market fueled by many factors. Many women who had relied on an enslaved workforce found themselves or their daughters lacking certain kitchen skills. Some books such as Fifty Years in a Maryland Kitchen (Mrs. B.C. Howard, 1877) and Mrs. Charles H. Gibson's Maryland And Virginia Cookbook (Mrs. C. H. Gibson, 1894) played into nostalgia for the antebellum era. Still others promoted a new interest in domestic science and nutrition. Over the course of the century, the role of many women changed from that of a "manager" of the kitchen, overseeing everything from bread-baking to home-brewing and animal slaughter, to a conscious consumer of those goods, and a steward of her family's health and happiness.

A lot of church groups published books to benefit charity.

Overall I think one of the primary drivers was just that it was a fun thing to do. Think of social media showing off pictures of what we eat. That's what these books are like – hundreds, sometimes thousands of recipes; often copied from other sources and completely untested; simply ideas about food.

Tracking down Maryland community cookbooks has become my obsession.

Every church cookbook is a historical document full of names – people who have backstories, and recipes that reflect the changing times. Through their recipes, people left a trail of information about their lives, aspirations and preferences. And all they were intending to do was have a good meal.

In my years of reading, writing and speaking about the food of my home state, I have come to believe that Maryland truly has a unique food culture unlike anywhere else.

We have Pennsylvania Dutch and German influences – scrapple, smearcase, peach cake, sauerkraut with Thanksgiving turkey. We have the Catholic traditions in Southern Maryland, where you can still get stuffed ham for Easter. Maple syrup from Western Maryland, and of course all the food from the Chesapeake Bay and its tributaries. When the first European explorers came here they were completely blown away by all of the food around them. Captain John Smith wrote of the bay, teeming with fish, "lying so thick with their heads above water, as for want of nets... [Smith and his men] attempted to catch them with a frying pan." (They were unsuccessful.)

We also have the Southern influence, the complicated baggage of that 'grand plantation cooking' that made its way into restaurants, hotels, and cookbooks. The food may be good but its origins can't be overlooked.

When I started a blog based on my recipe database, I committed myself to two years. As of this writing I am coming up on eight - with no end in sight. ❊

Broiled Chicken Deluxe, Edna Karlik

Posted on January 19, 2021

Mrs. Ronie Venables made honorable-mention in the first annual "National Chicken Cooking Contest" at the Delmarva Chicken Festival in 1949. Were she able to prepare her fried chicken on a wood-burning stove, she told a Universal Press reporter, she could have beaten out Mrs. A.L. Karlik for first place. The Press reporter contrasted the two contestants by describing Karlik as "pretty [and] young," and referring to Venables as a "70-year old farm woman."

In that article, Venables shared her prize-winning recipe in vague terms:

"A chicken, salt, pepper, egg, milk, flour and shortening. She stews the chicken, seasons it, dips it in a mixture of egg, milk and flour then fries it."

She declared that "the secret... is in putting the water in which the chicken is stewed on the chicken after it is fried."

For her part, Mrs. Karlik told the Wilmington, Delaware News-Journal that she was "flabbergasted" to have beat out the other 140 contestants. Family and friends had persuaded Karlik to enter the competition. She triumphed with "Broiled Chicken Deluxe," a recipe that she frequently made for her husband and 10-year old son.

You might think that Karlik and Venables would walk off into the sunset, Karlik with her prize-money and deep-freezer, and Venables with a fun memory, but that isn't exactly what happened. Cooking contests may seem blasé today, but the Delmarva Chicken Festival and the accompanying cooking contest were a big deal.

For Edna Karlik, the memory of her victory would resurface again and again.

Newspapers all over the country covered the 1949 contest. The Tampa, Florida Times reported that Mrs. Karlik "couldn't cook a lick when she married 14 years ago," and that she'd learned the recipe from an insurance agent. The Suburban List of Essex Junction, Vermont categorically declared "the best way to cook a chicken was determined in the first national cooking contest," and shared the "Broiled Chicken Deluxe" recipe with readers.

At the 1950 Delmarva Chicken Festival, Karlik presented the first prize to her successor Mrs. Talcie Howell. In 1954, Karlik was voted the head of the Wicomico County Council of Homemakers, and her recipe was in the Salisbury news once again. In 1959, the "National Father's Day Committee" declared Broiled Chicken Deluxe to be "the official recipe of Father's Day." Governor J. Millard Tawes presented Karlik with a citation and a plaque. In 1963, she attended the Chicken Festival in an official capacity, giving tips to that years' contestants.

Eventually, the National Chicken Cooking Contest was held outside of the Delmarva peninsula. It was "national," after all. The Wilmington Delaware Morning News covered the event in 1973. Karlik's win was again mentioned, along with the fact that although the event was held in Birmingham, Alabama, the winner had been a woman from Delaware. Chicken remained the pride of Delmarva.

As the years went on, the winning recipes changed with the times, incorporating a broader range of flavors, preparations and presentations. Many winners came and went, but Mrs. A.L. Karlik always reigned as the first.

She was born Edna May Hilfrank in Castleton-on-Hudson, New York in 1903. She married Albert Karlik in 1935. Before winning the National Chicken Cooking Contest, Edna's name appeared in the Salisbury Daily Times in 1946 because she found a dead body. Mrs. Karlik lived in Salisbury for most of her married life, and died in 1987. Posthumously, her name remained associated with the festival when the Salisbury Daily Times covered it's 50th anniversary in 1999, and in 2008 when the festival returned to Salisbury.

For Mrs. Karlik, the contest was her 'big break,' but Mrs. Venables still got her moments in the spotlight. The day after the Chicken Cooking Contest, she was interviewed about her competition experience and her life. She expressed her dislike of electric stoves, confessing to owning one that she never used. That article was syndicated and ran in papers like the Daily News in Dayton Ohio.

In 1961 Venables posed for the Salisbury Daily Times with her grandchildren and her Thanksgiving turkey. The caption declared that, as one of the original Chicken Contest winners, she had "a claim to fame in poultry roasting circles."

In 1969, at age 91, she was interviewed by the Times again. She had stayed up until 1 a.m. to watch the Moon landing. "It's God's plan to bring the world closer to God," she said, and expressed certainty that astronauts would one day visit Mars.

The final Delmarva Poultry Festival was held in 2014, years after many of the original cooking contestants had passed away. The Delmarva Poultry Industry recorded many of the recipes in several souvenir cookbooks. The recipes demonstrate the creativity and determination of several generations of home cooks, from a time when a chicken recipe could change a life. ❃

Broiled Chicken Deluxe

2 to 2.5 lb broiler-fryer, split
1 halved lemon
2 Teaspoons salt
.25 Teaspoon black pepper
.5 Teaspoons paprika
.5 Cup melted butter
2 Teaspoons sugar

Wipe chicken as dry as possible. Rub entire surface of chicken with cut lemon, squeezing out some juice. Sprinkle with mixture of salt, pepper, and paprika. Coat with melted butter, then sprinkle with sugar.
Place chicken in broiler pan and flatten pieces out. Place in broiler as far away from heat as possible, and cook 35 to 40 minutes. Baste occasionally with butter.

Recipe adapted from "Prize Winning Del-Mar-Va-Lous Chicken Recipes 1949 & 1950",
Delmarva Poultry Industry, 1950

Maryland Eggnog

From "Festive Maryland Recipes"

"Christmas comes but once a year, when eggnog takes the place of beer." – 1918

These days, Christmastime can feel tainted by materialism, compulsory spending, thoughtless gifts, and waste. Greedy corporations manipulate our nostalgia with limited edition Coke cans and the like. But there was a time, over a century ago, when things were simple and pure. Back in those days, before the Black Friday sales or department store extravaganzas, the Christmas holidays were more grounded, centered in the true reason for the season: getting #$@%*! up.

Make no mistake – our agrarian ancestors indeed worked their fingers to the bone day in, day out for the most of the year. But when winter rolled around, the harvests were put up, and the hogs had been killed and cured, one of the primary duties to attend to was partying. Families would travel or host visitors. When possible, food was shared in all directions. Spirits were consumed, often to excess. The large quantities called for in old eggnog recipes hearken to a time when a huge batch was made in late November to serve to guests throughout the season.

This annual cycle remained in the social DNA even as the nature of work changed, and more and more people flocked to cities and manned machines year round (or sat in offices and collected on the work of others). In this environment, things could get a little chaotic.

Especially in the rough-and-tumble environment of late 1800s Baltimore, the winter holidays correlated with a time of increased accidents, petty crimes, and some not-so-petty crimes.

In old newspapers, I found accounts of several incidents of murder or drugging by eggnog. The ubiquitous holiday beverage with its potent combination of liquors must have been a tempting vehicle for sinister motives in December.

More innocuously, eggnog was generally associated with the type of rowdiness that drew the finger-wagging of the temperance movement and the cautioning of elders. In 1890, two Baltimore men, aged 19 and 21, successfully used "egg-nogg" as a defense when they went to trial for stealing a horse and buggy on a lark.

Each year, news editorials appeared, admonishing would-be eggnog hellions to stop the insanity. In 1905, a Baptist reverend took to the pages of the Afro-American to decry the debauchery, firecrackers, and revealing clothing associated with Christmas revelry. Many young men, he warned, have their "lives blotted out" on this one day, and many young women "start to hell."

"The enjoyments of the Christmas festival were accompanied, as usual, with the usual number of accidents, some resulting from the careless use of firearms, whilst others may perhaps be attributed to the too free use of "egg-nogg and apple toddy." – Baltimore Sun, 1868

During the holiday season, temperance advocates gladly took on the title of "Anti Egg-Nog Movement" when holding meetings.

Still, the popularity of eggnog continued right on up to —and through— Prohibition. In 1921, the Sun declared that "eggnog is properly seasoned with real Jamaica rum, bootlegged at $8 a quart."

Although it was blamed for sowing mayhem, eggnog had its defenders. When in 1910 the Annapolis Capital paper quipped, "With eggs at 42 cents per dozen the Mint Julep Association is glad it does not belong to the Eggnog Clan," the Baltimore Sun indignantly reprinted the comment with a reply. "Clan, sister? It is a hierarchy, a universal brotherhood, a winged saraband that measures its membership by the millions and counts its kingdoms by the stars." ❀

Egg-nogg

12 eggs, separated
3 pints cream
2 pints milk
1.25 pints brandy (peach if you can find it, apple is the likely option)

.5 pints Jamaican rum
.5 pints Bourbon
9 oz sugar (or to taste)
nutmeg (optional)
1 tsp vanilla extract (optional)

Beat eggs until smooth and yellow. Gradually beat in sugar, followed by liquors, vanilla (if using) and finish with milk and cream. Optional: top with beaten egg whites or fold them in last. Top with nutmeg if desired.

Harvey Wallbanger Cake, Elaine Burns

A different version appeared in Eaten magazine 2019 issue No. 5: "Surf & Turf"

In the early 1970s, a popular new drink began to make appearances in advertisements and nightlife coverage.

Charles McHarry of the New York Daily News reported in his "On The Town" column:

"La Seine now has a drink called the Harvey Wallbanger, an import from Malibu, and here is how it was born: Seems a surfer known as Harvey bounced into a Malibu pub one night after a heavy day of hanging ten. He asked for a screwdriver and then as an afterthought asked the bartender to float an once and a half of Galliano on it. He finished the portion and promptly walked into the nearest wall. Hence Harvey Wallbanger, and it is not recommended at a lunch of less than two hours."

Similarly, Mickey Porter of the Ohio Akron Journal announced that the Brown Derby bar would be "the first in the area to feature the Harvey Wallbanger, a drink imported from Malibu, and here's how it was born..." You can guess the rest.

1960s tiki-bar culture was fading from favor, but a few elements survived. Among them were surfers and juice-based cocktails. Enter an intriguing imported liquor in a cool bottle, plus a bit of advertising ingenuity, and you have a mixture as potent as the Harvey Wallbanger itself: Galliano became the most-imported liquor of the 1970s.

Depending on how you look at it, the legend of the origin of the Harvey Wallbanger cocktail has been uncovered over the years – or just sured up to incorporate the available facts. Donato "Duke" Antone is said to have originated the drink around 1952 at a Los Angeles Bar called the Blackwatch. Some critics point out that Antone has been credited with a suspicious number of famed cocktails, including the Harvey Wallbanger, Rusty Nail, and the White Russian. To be fair, the enterprising WWII vet and former shoe-shine boy had won his share of awards in mixology. In the 1960s he operated a bartending school in Hartford Connecticut.

(He was also working as a consultant for Galliano at this time...) His fame made Hartford "the mixology capital of the world," according Antone's 1992 obituary in the the Hartford Courant.

There was a bar named the Black Watch on Sunset Boulevard – it closed in 1950. A subsequent Black Watch restaurant was opened by a Bob Feagon around that time on Las Tunas in Temple City. Advertisements and articles suggest dancing, cocktails – and a very upscale location. What was a surfer doing banging his head on a wall of a fancy restaurant miles inland? And who asks for "an once and a half of Galliano" as an "afterthought?" Even the stories that connect Duke Antone to a 'Blackwatch' restaurant in Los Angeles tend to arrive at the one loose end: the surfer, 'Tom Harvey', may never have existed.

The character of Tom Harvey is now generally attributed to ad-man Bill Young, hired by marketing director George Bednar of McKesson Imports company to promote one of their imports – Galliano. Young created a cartoon mascot and a slogan to promote the trendy cocktail: "Harvey Wallbanger is the name. And I can be made!"

If the Harvey Wallbanger cocktail was popularized by surfer mystique, that was certainly not capitalized on by Young's cartoons. Throughout the successful ad campaign, Harvey was portrayed as unsmiling and baggy-eyed, with a few strands of frazzled hair pointing from his round head. Whether surfing, skydiving, or running for president, his eyes conveyed uncomfortable alarm. At perhaps his most desperate, he is shown wearing a sandwich board with his namesake drink's recipe. "Harvey Wallbanger Is the Name...," he says to the reader. "Want to make something out of it?" His expression implies that he hopes you do not.

Although the Harvey Wallbanger cocktail had mostly faded from memory by the 1980s, it lived on in the form of a cake. The leap from the cocktail glass to cake-pan is not well documented. It may well have been another play from the liquor marketing camp. Recipes began to make the rounds not long after the cocktail itself in the early 1970s.

All of the earliest printed recipes for Harvey Wallbanger cake involve cake mix rather than a scratch-made cake. The popularity of the recipe was certainly a boon for Galliano, Dunkan Hines, and the Florida Citrus Commission.

On the other hand, there has never been a lack of inventive home cooks ready to incorporate trends into their baking. It's not such an unusual leap – alcohol has been used to flavor cakes for centuries. A very similar "Pennsylvania Dutch Orange Cake" predates the Harvey Wallbanger cake, although the ingredients vary – including the liqueur. Cake historian Laura Shapiro speculates "It's always been open season on cake mixes, and the manufacturers like it that way... People figured out ways to make the cakes themselves better or at least more interesting. My guess is that the Harvey Wallbanger version came from a liquor company, but you never know – people get very imaginative when they're using cake mixes."

Throughout the 70s, 80s and 90s, Harvey Wallbanger Cake recipes continued to be shared in newspaper columns and community cookbooks, even winning the occasional baking contest. A recipe for the cake was included in "Potato Chip Cookies and Tomato Soup Cake: Recipes of Americana" by Carole Everly in 1992.

In 1990, a reader of the News Journal in Wilmington Delaware requested the cake recipe in Nancy Coale Zippe's "What's Cooking" column. Zippe was wowed when she received a "record breaking" 59 replies. In her next column, she printed the names of each person who submitted a Harvey Wallbanger Cake recipe. People from all over Delaware had replied, plus a few surprise submissions from as far away as Arizona. The recipe that Zippe ultimately printed was credited to Chicago bartender Danny Lee McGuire, who "shared his idea" for a Harvey Wallbanger cake with Better Homes and Gardens in 1973. It may have been his idea, but he wasn't the first: newspapers had already been printing recipes for the cake based on the cocktail for at least a year... with the exact same ingredients.

Recipe columnists often referred to the cake recipe as "lost" or nostalgic, despite its consistent recurrence. Throughout all this, the recipe itself changed very little. When Dunkan Hines Orange Supreme cake mix became hard to find in the late 80s, bakers substituted lemon cake mix. Eventually, yellow cake became the standard.

In 1989, Remy Cointreau purchased Galliano and altered the 93 year old recipe. When Lucas Bols later acquired Galliano and reverted to the original recipe in 2010, memories of the Harvey Wallbanger cocktail resurfaced. Liquor.com declared the cocktail "a modern classic." Saveur writer Robert Simonson absolved the Harvey Wallbanger of the bad reputation the cocktail had earned as "one of the preeminent drinks of the 1970s... a time of sloppy, foolish drinks."

The cake, of course, has had a few "from scratch" revisions, but the cake mix version continues to reappear wherever there's a recipe-finder column. And with the ability to order the elusive "Orange Supreme" cake mix online, purists are in luck. The real surfer named Harvey may never surface... but he can be made. ❁

Harvey Wallbanger Cake

1 package orange cake mix
1 (3 3/4 oz) package pudding mix
4 eggs
.5 Cups cooking oil
.5 Cup orange juice
.5 Cup Galliano
2 Tablespoons vodka
Glaze:

1 Cup sifted powdered sugar
1 Tablespoon orange juice
1 Tablespoon Galliano
1 Teaspoon vodka
In large bowl, combine cake mix and pudding. Add eggs, oil, 1/2 c. orange juice, 1/2 c. Galliano and 2 T. vodka.Beat on low speed for 1/2 min. beat on med. speed 5 min. Pout into greased and floured 10 in. fluted tube pan. Bake at 350° for 45 min. Cool for 10 min. in pan, remove to rack and pour on glaze while cake is warm.Glaze-combine last 4 ingredients listed above.

Recipe from "Loyola Recipes", Loyola Mothers' Club, 1974

Gumbo Filé, M. E. M'Ilhenny, Avery Island, Louisiana

Posted on June 7, 2022

"Gumbo Filet Powder is made of the tender young leaves of the sassafras," wrote Jane Gilmor Howard in her 1873 cookbook Fifty Years in A Maryland Kitchen, "picked in the Spring, and dried carefully in the shade as you do herbs; powdered fine, bottled and corked tight. It is much used in New Orleans."

This explanation was doing one better than Howard's relative Mary Lloyd Tyson had done in her 1870 cookbook The Queen of the Kitchen. Tyson's recipe, for "Gumbo Fillet," didn't presume that the ingredient needed any explaining. "Stir in 1 table-spoon of fillet, if it is fresh," she wrote, "if not, put 2."

Howard copied many recipes from The Queen of the Kitchen, but this was not one of them. Tyson's recipe was pretty open-ended. She suggested readers add "as many oysters as you please" and advised that "Gumbo can be made of either ducks, pigeons, or cold turkey." Jane Howard settled on a quart of oysters and a chicken.

Gumbo recipes containing okra are plentiful in Maryland cookbooks and recipe manuscripts dating back to the early 1800s, but Gumbo Filé is a bit of a specialty item. Elizabeth Ellicott Lea included an okra gumbo in her 1859 book Domestic Cookery, but as far as she knew or cared, sassafras was best used in a poultice (also containing bread crumbs and milk. If you have a flesh wound you might want to steer clear of Lea.)

When Tyson presented "Gumbo Fillet" in Queen of the Kitchen, she commented "This is a favorite dish in the Southern States."

This may be an example of the mystique of antebellum cooking and lifestyle that was implied in the recipes of Tyson and Howard, who both had plenty of Confederate ties. In 1898, Mrs. W. A. Fisher contributed a recipe each for gumbo with filé and okra for Recipes Old and New, a cookbook produced to benefit the Confederate Relief Bazaar.

While one theory of the origin of the name "gumbo" traces the word to West African words for okra, in the language of the Choctaw people, sassafras powder is called "kombo." That raises too much confusion for me to write much more about gumbo at present.

What attracted me to this recipe was the name signed at the bottom of the page on which it was written.

The Frick Family Papers collection at the Maryland Center for History and Culture contains numerous recipe books and loose scrap collections. A lot of the recipe collection is associated with Jane "Jeannie" Turnbull, who lived in Washington DC from 1841-1912. Though Turnbull remained unmarried throughout her life, she seems to have been something of a socialite, who was invited to receptions and dances at embassies and at the White House.

Sifting through the Turnbull recipe collection, I was greeted with a variety of recipes written in bound books, newspaper clippings, and scraps of paper typed or handwritten by family friends and acquaintances. Many of the names are vague or the handwriting illegible, but there were three recipes – for "Jumbalaya!," Terrapin, and Gumbo Filé with an elaborate signature at the bottom: "M. E. M.Ilhenny, Avery Island, La."

Mary Eliza McIlhenny was born Mary Eliza Avery in 1838 to Sarah Marsh Avery and Daniel Dudley Avery, who was a Baton Rouge lawyer, state senator, judge, and sugar planter. (You could wonder how someone could be so accomplished if you momentarily forget that the family enslaved a bunch of people.) In 1859, Mary Eliza married one of her father's business associates, Edmund McIlhenny, a banker who was originally from Hagerstown Maryland.

McIlhenny family lore is plentiful, but often poorly substantiated. Edmund McIlhenny's great-grandfather is said to have immigrated from Ireland in the 1740s, with the family origins tracing back to Scotland.

In America, the McIlhennys established themselves around southeastern Pennsylvania.

Edmund's father John, born in 1780, ended up in Maryland when he "eloped" with Ann Newcomer. Tabasco: An Illustrated History by Shane Bernard, mentions that Ann was said to be "a Baltimore girl." Other genealogies online put her birth around Lancaster Pennsylvania.

One family tree shows Ann having five siblings, including a sister, Elizabeth, who married John McIlhenny's brother, Joseph. Joseph and Elizabeth appear on Washington County censuses and marriage lists.

Considering the two parallel family marriages and close residence, John and Anns "elopement" seems a little dramatic.

At any rate, John and Ann settled in Hagerstown around 1810. John operated a tavern that advertised availability to "Genteel Boarders," and was also involved in politics and banking. Edmund, the second of nine brothers, was born in 1815.

After his father died in 1832, Edmund left Hagerstown, and possibly spent some time in Baltimore before moving to Louisiana. In 1859, Edmund married Mary Eliza Avery.

I couldn't find any apparent connection between the Averys/ McIlhennys and the Turnbulls/Fricks, but if there was one, it probably came about in Louisiana rather than Maryland. Edmund McIlhenny may have spent a few years in Baltimore, but he didn't really make his fortunes until he lived in down South.

Jane Turnbull's father, Col. William Turnbull, was in New Orleans as an engineer to build a customs house in 1848-1849.

It's most likely that the recipe made it's way from Mary Eliza McIlhenny to Jeannie Turnbull through the social networks of their generally Confederate-sympathizing families. Its hard to ever know who was acquainted and how. The recipes themselves are one clue.

Although I found a few references to Mary Eliza's own handwritten recipe manuscript, none of her recipes are publicly available for comparison. When I shared my images with Shane Bernard, he wrote that he "immediately recognized the handwriting as Mary Eliza's."

If this essay seems a little disjointed, I am aware. Think of the whole as an orphaned footnote to some larger story. There's simply too much to delve into in the vast Frick Family Papers, the McIlhenny and Averys, the people that these families enslaved, and of course the pre-history and rise of Tabasco Sauce, Edmund McIlhenny's product that left an unlikely legacy. It's a murky mix, not unlike gumbo. ❀

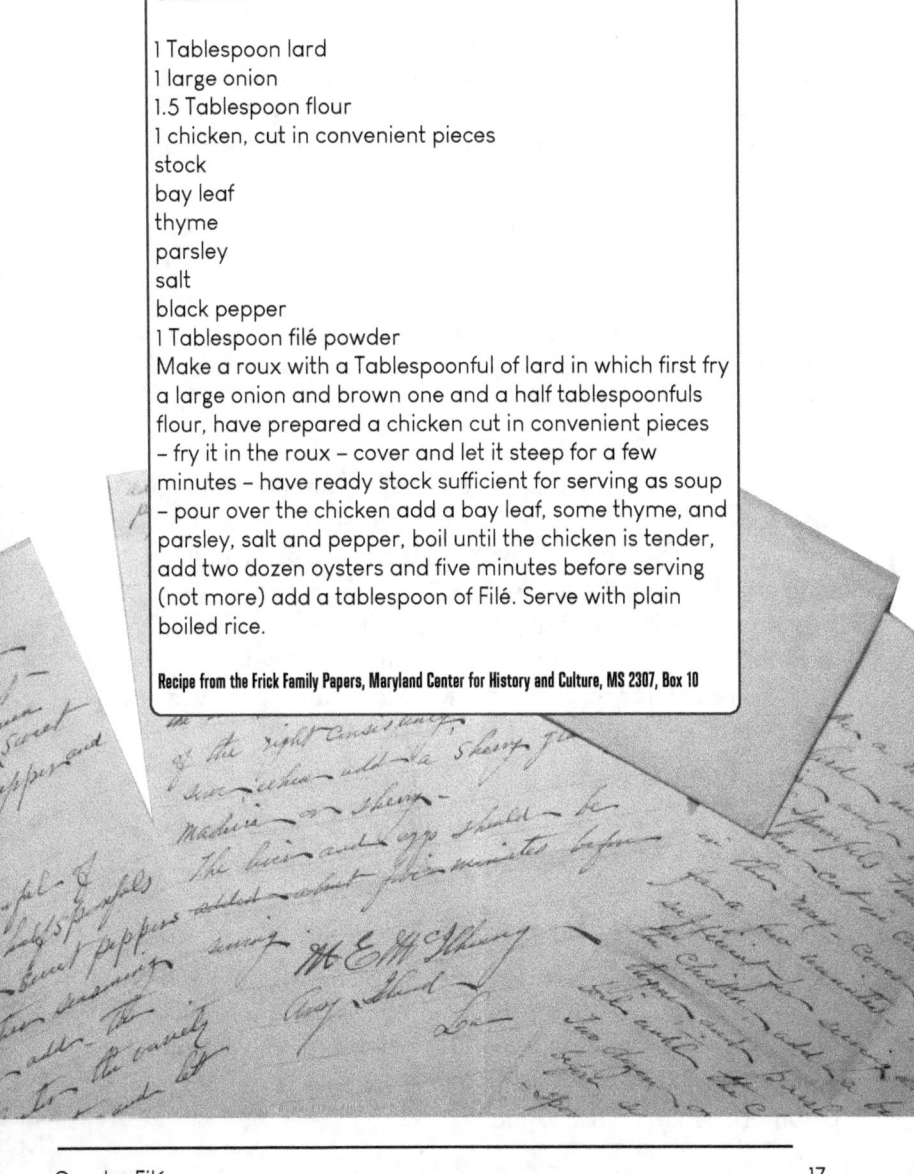

Gumbo Filé

1 Tablespoon lard
1 large onion
1.5 Tablespoon flour
1 chicken, cut in convenient pieces
stock
bay leaf
thyme
parsley
salt
black pepper
1 Tablespoon filé powder

Make a roux with a Tablespoonful of lard in which first fry a large onion and brown one and a half tablespoonfuls flour, have prepared a chicken cut in convenient pieces – fry it in the roux – cover and let it steep for a few minutes – have ready stock sufficient for serving as soup – pour over the chicken add a bay leaf, some thyme, and parsley, salt and pepper, boil until the chicken is tender, add two dozen oysters and five minutes before serving (not more) add a tablespoon of Filé. Serve with plain boiled rice.

Recipe from the Frick Family Papers, Maryland Center for History and Culture, MS 2307, Box 10

Egg Flake Soup, Henri Casalegno

Posted on September 19, 2019

The Baltimore Sun advertised in April of 1909 that they would be running two features in their Sunday editions, with soup recipes from M. Henri Casalegno, a former chef at the Maryland Club. That credential was apt to make Baltimore housewives pay attention. H.L. Mencken certainly knew that when he gave the chef the freelance writing assignments. Mencken later recalled that the Italian-born chef's articles were "done in very fair English."

Casalegno did not apparently hold the "housewife cook" in high regard. "The failures of the housewife cook are often due to her failure properly to season the food she cooks," he wrote. To be fair to Casalegno, a preachy condescending tone was the norm for cookery advice of the day. Casalegno may simply have been embellishing his prowess by emulating others. It wouldn't be the last time he did so.

Casalagno had been working as a chef in hotel kitchens since his arrival in the U.S. in 1904. In his first stateside position at the Hotel Renssalaer in Troy, New York, he'd had a quarrel with another chef, Paul Lescaux. The altercation resulted in Lescaux's death. According to Casalagno, Lescaux had lunged at him, landing with a knife in the heart. Casalagno served four years in prison for this "accident," before finding his way into the Maryland Club and the Baltimore Sun columns.

What came after is somehow even more bizarre.

Casalegno moved to New York and began to go by the name Henry Woodhouse (a translation of his Italian name). In Woodhouse's new life, he conjured up lofty credentials in the then relatively new field of aviation.

He went on to write countless articles about aviation and built a name as a foremost expert. He helped found the American Society of Aeronautic Engineering. He wrote books on aviation and expressed prescient opinions on the use of aircraft in commerce, mail delivery, and war.

In 1920, there was a lot of drama within the Aero Club of America, of which Henry was an early and influential member. Factions split, lawsuits were filed, Henry made some questionable claims (including possibly forging 400 signatures to sway a vote), and eventually, he was shamed with the resurrection of his criminal past.

A pariah in the aviation world, Woodhouse moved on to oil speculation. He formed a syndicate called the Ottoman American Development Company to procure oil from Turkey. Ultimately, he probably didn't profit much due to political turmoil and divisions in Turkey. That fact didn't stop him from bragging:

"In later years, Woodhouse inflated this episode to Herman Herst Jr., a philatelic authority and fellow collector. 'Another one of my big coups was when I utilized a little fact I picked up from the Bible. I had read a biblical tale about fire shooting out of the earth in Mesopotamia. That meant only one thing to me—oil! I talked Standard Oil into looking into the matter and of course they discovered oil. They gave me a royalty from every barrel taken out of the Near East oil fields.'" – "I'm Working on a Million Dollar Deal": A Biographical Essay on Henry Woodhouse by Jerry Kuntz

Woodhouse was a multifaceted man with interests beyond oil, aviation, and cooking. He was also an avid collector of American historical artifacts, particularly those associated with George Washington. Many of his Washington-related collections were donated to the Library of Congress. The Henry Woodhouse collection contains letters, maps, land grants and more relating to the first President of the United States. While most of these items are legitimate, Woodhouse may have sold some artifacts of more questionable origin. He worked with a Washington descendant, W. Lanier Washington, to add the family crest to items for sale. He also worked with a painter of fake portraits.

Perhaps the longest-running interest in Woodhouse's life, from his aviation days to his twilight years, was litigation. He'd threatened the Aero Club of America with legal action. He copyrighted aviation terms and successfully sued the creators of the Clara Bow movie "Wings" for $25,000. In the 1950s, he tried to sue General Electric for stealing ideas that he'd suggested by mail. Around the same time, he counter-sued an employee of his who was suing him for wage theft. He claimed the woman, Tamara Bourkoun, was using him to get to his prominent clients to offer them fortune-telling services. The cases dragged on for years. The court ruled with Bourkoun.

When Woodhouse died in 1970, he had over thirty-five pending lawsuits.

The Egg Flake Soup, by the way, is fine. Any soup like this is going to taste as good as the broth you use. The recipe is very similar to Stracciatella, a soup from Woodhouse's home country of Italy. Among the other recipes he shared in the Sun are recipes for pea soup, vegetable soup, barley soup, [French] onion soup, as well as the more Maryland-centric oyster and crab soups. Whether they came from Henri's own mind, the Maryland Club or -who knows?- the unfortunate chef who fell on Woodhouse's knife that fateful day, the M. Henri Casalegno soup recipes are an interesting side note in varied and unusual life. ❋

Egg Flake Soup:

"This soup can be made in 10 minutes and is just the thing when company arrives unexpectedly; Flavor four cups of boiling water with meat extract and bring to a boil. Beat well in a bowl three eggs; pour them in the soup; let stand one minute for the eggs to cook; then stir well to break the eggs into flakes. Season to taste with salt and pepper and serve very hot. On account of the eggs and the beef extract, a teaspoonful of which is equivalent to one pound of meat, this soup is very nourishing. Egg flake soup can also be made with fresh beef or chicken broth; then the meat extract should be omitted."

Recipe from the Baltimore Sun, "The Secrets of Good Soup Making" by Henri Casalegno, ["Late of the Maryland Club"], April 4, 1909

By Henri Casalegno.
[Late of the Maryland Club.]

SOUP is considered the prelude of every dinner by those people whose menu runs up to fine courses. To people of limited means, however, it is more than that. Indeed, they often find soup and a little something else quite sufficient for a meal.

Henri Casalegno

Unfortunately, few housewives know how to make good soup and inexpensively. Therefore, to have soup at their tables more than once or twice a week would mean a Waterloo to the weekly income and a tax on their patience.

A History of Crab Cakes

Posted on September 28, 2017

Here in Baltimore, the ever-booming crabcake trade props up more than just restaurants and tourism. Advertisers make embarrassing attempts to appeal to our obsession. There's documentaries about the search for the best crab cake. And more and more, our local publications are fishing for clicks by urging people to vote for the region's best crabcake.

Everyone is compelled to have a favorite. Some are loyal to tradition, standing by Faidley's and accepting no imitators. Others take pride in preferring something newer and better – the old standard simply won't do.

There's an unspoken commonality to all contenders for 'Baltimore's Best Crab Cake': they must be jumbo lump. Anything less is perceived as unworthy of consideration; a rip-off; an insult. The fact that this requirement elevates our most beloved food item to a luxury seems beside the point. The truly knowledgeable must be willing and able to indulge enough so as to have an opinion which is the best among them.

To be perfectly honest, I stopped taking this plunge years ago. I rarely had a crabcake worth the price of admission. The best crabcakes are made at home. And of those, the very very best... turned out to not be jumbo lump meat at all.

I've been wielding this contrarian opinion for awhile now, intending to eventually compose the rant you are reading now. But when I began to do a little background research into just when this jumbo lump madness began, I got more than I bargained for. I ended up back at the origin of the crab cake itself; sifting through legends and lies.

One oft-repeated yarn about the origin of the crabcake is that the Native Americans of the Chesapeake region made their crab cakes with cornmeal, and fried them in bear fat. This story comes from "Chesapeake" by James Michener, a fictional novel (redundancy intentional). Michener is remembered for his extensive research and attention to detail, but he's no culinary historian.

I reviewed documents from Captain John Smith accounts and "A Briefe Relation of the Voyage unto Maryland" by Father Andrew White, to the works of anthropologist Helen Rountree and I found no accounts of foodways remotely resembling the method described in "Chesapeake."

Finally, I reached out to folklorist Bernard Herman, who has made a study of Eastern Shore native and early settler foodways. He had a lot of input which I may as well quote verbatim:

"Let's start with fried foods. Frying requires both oil and a utensil that can withstand high heat. Skillets and frying pans appear in the earliest estate records on the Eastern Shore of Virginia with references dating to the 1630s (the public records here are the oldest continuous records in the US – unbroken from 1632). So we know that the capacity for frying foods dates to the earliest European and African presence. As far as I know, there is not a frying component to the cuisines of first peoples – the scant record suggesting that the armature of their foodways centered on "stews" (understood here as one-pot dishes), roasted, or dried/preserved preparations. Thus, my first reaction... is that the crab cake is something that is most likely not a product of indigenous foodways.

Now to the crab cake itself. The crabcake at its heart is a kind of fritter – and fritters have a very complex history. "Cake" in this case describes a pan-fried fritter – not unlike oyster cakes. The fritter traditions of the Chesapeake are the product of what the great food historian Jessica Harris terms a "braided tradition" a coming together of many cultural strands. Michael Twitty, for example, describes African fritter traditions in circulation in the 18th-c. Virginia and Maryland."

It seems that the notion that we are engaging in an eons-old tradition when we eat a crabcake may be a bit of romantic embellishment.

The labor-intensive step of picking crabs for crabcakes, like our beaten biscuits, recalls instead the other major injustice that our state was founded on, and the fact that, as Michael Twitty put it, in Fighting Old Nep: Foodways of Enslaved Afro-Marylanders,

---

1634-1864, "the plantation was a training ground for a future life of serving high society."

Other accounts state that "it was not until 1930 in Crosby Gaige's New York World's Fair cook book that the term 'crab cake' appears in print, where it referred to the delicacy as 'Baltimore crab cake.'"

I am not sure how this demonstrable falsehood can continue to circulate in the google age, but so-named recipes appeared at least as early as 1891. That year, Thomas Jefferson Murrey included a recipe for "Crab Cakes" in his book "Cookery with a Chafing Dish."

> **Crab Cakes.**—The meat from the hard shell crabs, after boiling, may be made into little cakes, held together with the yolk of an egg, seasoned with salt and pepper, then cooked on both sides in the chafing dish with a small amount of butter or oil.

Murrey was a New York caterer famous for seafood – his nickname was "Terrapin Tom" – and he had also worked in Washington, DC. It may be worth noting that eleven years earlier, his 1880 book "Valuable Cooking Receipts" contains a suggested menu provided by "a patriotic son of Maryland" in which crabcakes are notably absent. Murrey was a celebrity epicure whose influence spread not only through the books he wrote but through his catering. He died by mysterious and sudden suicide in 1900.

In 1894, a recipe appeared in "Mrs. Charles Gibson's Maryland and Virginia Cook Book" for "Crab Cakes for Breakfast":

> **CRAB CAKES FOR BREAKFAST. (Very nice.)**
>
> Take the crab after it is picked and season it high with red pepper and salt. Then add butter, and make them in round cakes, using a little flour to hold them together. Then dip them in egg and cracker beaten fine. Fry in hot butter or lard.

Even before the published recipes, crab cakes are mentioned in newspapers. An 1873 tidbit in the Harrisburg Telegraph raved excitedly that a new establishment, The Harris House, offered a bill of fare including "everything that can be desired" such as meats of all kinds, asparagus, stewed turtle, "ice cream of different flavors," hard shell crabs, deviled crabs, and "crab cakes."

To be fair, there is a possibility that the crab cakes in the Harris House might not have been like the crabcakes we eat today. In 1901, chef H. Franklyn Hall wrote a definitive seafood cookbook for the era, "300 Ways to Cook and Serve Shell Fish." Born in Washington DC in 1853, Hall serves as a prime example of the fame and success that Black chefs could hope to enjoy through the cooking and catering trades at the turn of the 20th century. At the time his book was published, he'd worked for some 30 years at hotels and restaurants in Rhode Island, New Jersey and Pennsylvania, and was currently working at the Boothby Hotel in Philadelphia.

"300 Ways to Cook and Serve Shell Fish" contains a crab cake. Hall's "Crab Cakes" were more like pancakes containing crabmeat:

> NO. 11.—CRAB CAKES, BUTTER SAUCE.
> Make a stiff, rich cake, batter thin, mix in enough crab meat to make stiff. Cook on gridiron or in a smooth bottom fry pan same as griddle or pan cakes; serve with drawn butter for breakfast or lunch.

The Harris House may well have served this other form of 'Crab Cake' from Pennsylvania, or it could be that the crabcake recipe we know today traveled to Harrisburg from Maryland, shipped along with the crabs themselves, up the Susquehanna River.

H. Franklyn Hall's book does contain a recipe for lobster or crab "cutlet". As Bernard Herman mentioned, the true crabcake lineage likely belongs in the fritter family. These recipes tend to be called "cutlets" or "patties". Lady Nugent, wife of a Governor of Jamaica (1801 to 1806) during the time when the island was under British rule and enslavement, wrote a diary in which she described the food of the colony. While she raved about a crab pepper-pot, she also passingly mentioned being served "flesh & fowl, crab patties &c &c" as part of a lavish dinner.

Across the seas in Edinburgh, a recipe appeared in Mrs. Williamson's 1849 "The Practice of Cookery and Pastry" for crab or lobster cutlets, the meat mixed with pepper, lemon pickle and gravy, made "in the form of lamb cutlets", breaded and fried, and served garnished with a crab claw.

In 1870, "Jennie June's American Cookbook" offered up one of those "from one housewife to another" cookbooks that we know and love to this day. In it, Jennie June's recipe for "Crab [or] Lobster Cutlets" stewed and seasoned crab meat in stock before mixing in flour and spices then breading and frying the cutlets.

These recipes appear to be bridging the divide between the modern form of crabcake and recipes dating back to Robert May's 1660 "To Stew Crabs" and Hannah Glasse's 1747 method "To Dress A Crab."

> ### To dreſs a Crab.
>
> HAVING taken out the Meat, and cleanſed it from the Skin, put it into a Stew-pan, with Half a Pint of White Wine, a little Nutmeg, Pepper and Salt, over a ſlow Fire. Throw in a few Crumbs of Bread, beat up one Yolk of an Egg with one Spoonful of Vinegar, throw it in, then ſhake the Sauce-pan round a Minute, and ſerve it up on a Plate.

Still, the relationship remained fast and loose for decades to come, with deviled crabs served in the shell retaining their popularity (and eventual influence on the crabcake formula) up until the early 1900's.

The Democratic Press in Columbus Ohio ran a lamentation about the popularity of deviled crab in 1883. "They are eaten by epicures, epicacs and other foreigners. They cost about fifty cents apiece, and are the least food for the most money extant," the angry writer declared. "Devilled crabs are never eaten in private. What is the use of a man mortgaging all his real estate to buy devilled crabs to eat when no one is looking at him?"

As early as 1835, "crabs could be marketed much more readily in the form of crab meat than in the shell". The demand for deviled crab still necessitated that the shells be sold in order to pack the meat back into.

The industry progressed slowly, especially with the much-more-economically-important oyster vying for resources. The Baltimore Sun reported that 1884 was a boom year for crab harvests – but that the crab picking business, which was "carried out in private residences" was "yet in its infancy." Interestingly it is noted that "when prepared by the regular pickers the meat is in larger pieces than it is when picked by the old-fashioned restaurants, and to many it is not so pleasing to the taste."

Over in Crisfield, the market for picked crab meat was still described as "of no importance" in 1891. Only two plants were hiring women to pick the meat, which was packed on ice in buckets and sent to hotels and restaurants. Crisfield was the number one source for blue crabs nationally at that time – with the trade occasionally escalating in violence to rival the oyster wars. In 1894 the Sun reported a rain of bullets "flying in every direction" at illegal crabbers in Dorchester County. The crabbers (plus a toddler they had sleeping onboard) made it out alive but were fined heavily and their boats confiscated.

The crab dogma that is inescapable in Maryland nowadays began to set in at this time. One indignant woman wrote to the Baltimore Sun to express outrage upon learning that Philadelphians were boiling crabs.

"I hardly have patience to tell those Philadelphians, but it may be good missionary work, that the way to get a dozen hard crabs ready for picking is to put them, alive, in a round pot over a good fire, pour half a pint of vinegar and a gill of water in the pot, cover up with wet seaweed if at hand, if not with ordinary fresh and green sod grass from the yards; if neither is accessible, with anything which will keep the steam in and let the vinegar steam cook the crabs. Boiled crab meat is not fit to be eaten. To use it in deviled crabs or croquettes spoils the whole dish." – A Talbot Lady's Indignation over a Philadelphia Recipe, Baltimore Sun, 1896

Mary Elizabeth Wilson Sherwood, who was born in New Hampshire but resided in Washington DC declared in "The Art of Entertaining" that "A devilled crab is considered good, but it should be cooked by a negro expert from Maryland."

The urban preference for crabcakes and deviled crab prepared outside the home could explain why so few recipes for these items exist in the 19th century cooking manuscripts collection of the Maryland Historical Society.

In the late 19th and early 20th century, many African Americans achieved financial success as caterers. The history is fraught - caterers were pigeonholed and fetishized in Maryland culinary culture. This took place in hotels, clubs, restaurants and private kitchens but also spilled out onto the streets of Baltimore as the "crab men" roamed the city with baskets of deviled crabs and crabcakes for sale. The Baltimore Sun lamented in 1905 that this tradition was dying out. The prices of supplies were rising, and white customers refused to pay the Black vendors more than 5 cents for their wares.

The sale of crab meat was becoming increasingly industrialized, and its terms codified. A 1905 book, "The Crab Industry of Maryland" described the classes of crab meat: flakes, ordinary, and "fat meat", "the flakes being considered much superior to the other because they are whiter and firmer." This is today's jumbo lump. All of this meat was still shipped with crab shells used in the serving of deviled crab.

Crabcakes had become a celebrated part of Maryland life, appearing in poetry in newspapers like the Frederick News and the Baltimore Sun. "Summertown," a 1910 poem by "The Benztown Bard" Folger McKinsey made an explicit association between the appreciation of crabcakes and the ambiance of the street vendor:

"Under an awning of canvas, striped, emerald, brown or red;
Watermelon, a cent a slice, cooling and tempting spread;
Mystical bell of the crabcake man wending his way along;

Chanting the lilt of the rhythmic rune borne of the crabcake song"

Advertisements for "lump" crab meat were making an appearance, with "flake" now relegated to second-class status. "Back Fin" still served as an alternate term for the desirable large chunks of crab meat. By the late 1930s, restaurants were advertising crabcakes that were "all lump."

In the early 1940's, a Baltimore Sun Columnist named John O' Ren got into a debate with a reader. The banter spanned over several columns. O'Ren considered whether 'Deviled crab a' la Maryland' was more about the ingredients, or the culture and economy surrounding it. He created a hierarchy of ways to enjoy crab: steamed crabs, deviled crabs, crab soup. He conceded fourth place to the crab cake, while the reader "Crabtown Cook" asserted that crab cakes "properly prepared" could be just as good as deviled crab. Eventually another reader chimed in to lament how much of O'Ren's column's space was being wasted on the topic of crabs.

The confusion over the grades of crab continued for some time. Local food authority of the 50s and 60s Virginia Roeder listed the types as "claw or dark," "regular white," "special white" and "backfin or deluxe" while her nationally syndicated counterpart Clementine Paddleford explained the classes as "lump," "flake" and "the brownish meat from the claws" which she said was preferred for cakes and to devil.

A later Baltimore Sun food writer, Rob Kasper, expressed dismay at the ongoing confusion in 1988. "As recently as five years ago, when you bought a package labeled 'backfin lump,' it was the king of the hill, top of line, the best meat the blue crab had to offer. Now instead of the top of the line, backfin is second, sometimes even third in line," yielding to lump and jumbo lump. Competition was shifting the terms towards the more descriptive. To this day, the terms remain arbitrary but have become more generally accepted.

My own bias against the jumbo lump hegemony was first backed up in the Sun as early as 1948, when Eastern-shoreman W.C. Mills shared his crabcake recipe which follows my own preference: "All the meat goes into one pile – claw, lump and flake," and with it the fat. "The fat makes all the difference in the world... packers can't ship it; it spoils too quickly." (Growing up, this is what we called the 'mustard'.)

Woodberry Kitchen's Spike Gjerde declared in 2011 that he "would love to be able to buy a whole-crab mix in a single container." ("Crab lovers: Can you get over the lump?", Baltimore Sun, 12/5/11) Having some celebrity chef plus food writer Richard Gorelick share my opinion made me feel credentialed, even if I'd been beaten to the punch.

Studying history is more like a day of snacking than a satisfying meal. Sure, I learned a lot of things were untrue, but what about truths? Where's the zinger? Did Terrapin Tom popularize the crab-cake? Did the preference for lump stem from the suspicions of fish or other adulterants in crabcakes sold on the street? Was the crabcake ever truly democratic or just another of unequal

Baltimore's elitist traditions?

There was no definitive culinary moment happening as the white man stole the land, the water, and the crabcake too. No Worlds Fair bringing the crabcake into the spotlight.

Crabcakes were made in many forms, and many hands, in bondage, in fancy hotels, in make-do kitchens. They've been made from claw meat, jumbo lump, with bread, no bread, seasoned or plain. These options have been alternately guided by gourmet preference and everyday necessity.

The story of our favorite regional dish may not be exceptional, but it is emblematic. ❈

CRAB CAKES I

1 pound crab meat

2 slices bread

1 egg, beaten

1 teaspoon Worcestershire sauce

1 tablespoon mayonnaise

2 teaspoons seafood seasoning

1 tablespoon snipped parsley

Pick over crab meat to remove shells. Remove crusts from bread, and break bread into small pieces. Mix bread with beaten egg. Add remaining ingredients. Form into cakes. Dip into cracker crumbs and saute quickly in a small amount of fat. 6 crab cakes.

30

Richard Q. Yardley from "Fun With Seafood," Virginia Roeder, 1960

Mrs. Kitching's Ham Potato Salad Loaf

Posted on August 31, 2019

Many home cooks dream of achieving what Emily Frances Kitching did. Kitching's Smith Island boardinghouse was no restaurant. Guests ate at a set time. Meals were served at communal dinner tables. There wasn't a menu to choose from – there was a smorgasbord of seafood soups or chowders; crab cakes; clam fritters; ham; hot rolls; stewed vegetables; pickled carrots; macaroni, bean or potato salads; corn pudding; iced tea. No one went hungry. Guests kept coming, and word spread. Frances Kitching achieved culinary fame on her own terms.

While some credit Kitching with the invention of Smith Island Cake, a recipe for the cake does not appear in the original 1981 edition of "Mrs. Kitching's Smith Island Kitchen." Still, there can be little debate that Kitching's food was synonymous with Smith Island cooking. What began as a way to feed the men who were installing electricity on the secluded island in the 1950s became a force that attracted outsiders to experience life on Smith Island.

In a 1981 Washington Post article about Mrs. Kitching, food writer Joan Nathan declared that "Frances Kitching is a slow starter in the kitchen," strolling into her world-famous kitchen with a cigarette, waiting until the last minute to prepare some fried fish. "The last minute is when she spies from her kitchen window the 'Captain Jason' ferry approaching," Nathan wrote.

Despite her stated requirement that guests provide advance notice of their expected party number, Kitching made sure that everyone who visited her was well fed. A 1978 review of Kitching's boardinghouse food, written by Kathy Canavan in the Wilmingon Delaware News Journal, described a busy Frances Kitching recovering from serving lunch to 18 guests when she'd expected four. "It would break my heart for someone to leave here and say they wasn't satisfied," she remarked. "It really would."

Reviews often wrote of the crab cakes, just one of many crab dishes served in a meal. Her soups and chowders – made with evaporated milk – were famous. Kitching's culinary oeuvre encompassed all courses of a meal down to her pickled carrots. In her cookbook, cooked carrots are marinated in a mixture of French dressing, tomato soup, mustard, paprika, vinegar and brown sugar. Visitors from the press almost always mentioned them. For dessert, she served homemade pies or cakes. She often used the figs and pomegranates that still grow on the island today.

Frances Kitching became so synonymous with Smith Island cooking that, when I visited the island in 2015, I detected that her rivalries with competing restauranteurs had outlived her. Kitching died in 2003 at the age of 84. Her boardinghouse had been closed for 16 years, but her reputation had hardly waned.

I recently made this "Ham Potato Salad Loaf" from her cookbook. I was drawn to its aspic-like composition. When I couldn't get the kind of ham that I prefer, I decided to go with the drama of laying out slices of ham instead of using chopped ham as per Mrs. Kitching's instructions. Despite my ridiculous presentation, the potato salad was well-liked. I don't think Mrs. Kitching would have approved of my shortcut. Nor would she approve of the beers I had alongside it. "[Drinkers] were in no condition to enjoy and appreciate good cooking," she was once quoted as saying.

Now that Smith Island Cake is the State Dessert of Maryland, Kitching's name lives on in relation to it, even if her invention of the cake is disputed. At any rate, it wasn't the cake that visitors wrote about. It was her many ways with the seafood that sustained the island's economy. It was her memorable personality – Kitching ensured that her guests were well fed and treated, but she did not suffer fools, or would-be violators of Smith Island's prohibition of alcohol – lightly. ❆

Ham Potato Salad Loaf

6 oz chopped ham
1 envelope gelatin
.5 Cup water
1 Cup mayonnaise
1 Teaspoon salt (& other seasonings to taste)
1 Teaspoon minced onion
.25 Cup parsley
.25 Teaspoon red and/or green pepper
4 stalk celery, diced
4 Cups cooked potato, diced

Line a 9 x 5-inch loaf pan with foil or lightly grease a similar-sized mold. Line the bottom and sides of the mold with ham. Dissolve gelatin in warm water. Gently stir together gelatin and remaining ingredients. Pack mixture into mold and chill until set. Turn out on to a cold platter. Garnish with lettuce and tomatoes.

Recipe adapted from "Mrs. Kitching's Smith Island Cookbook" by Frances Kitching and Susan Stiles Dowel

Ham Potato Salad Loaf

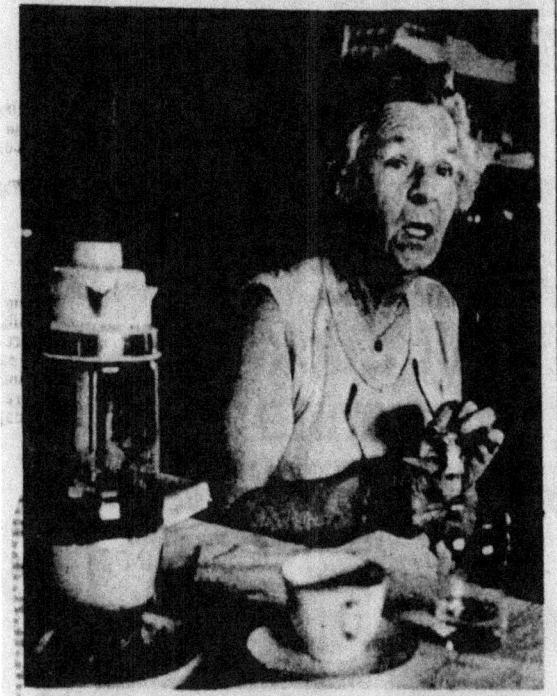

Evening Journal, Wilmington, Del., Wednesday, October 11, 1978 · · · **43**

Staff Photo by Chuck McGowen

Frances Kitching

Her Rooming House Is for True Lovers Of Home Cooking

Hard Jelly Cake

Posted on December 25, 2020

When I finally took a stab at baking the Shady Side specialty Hard Jelly Cake in 2020, I nervously wondered how my reputation would fare.

Treading in the steps of experts is always a setup for embarrassment. If my beaten biscuit experience taught me anything, it's that the flame-keepers of some of our state's more forgotten foods tend to take their responsibility seriously. When my attempt cast disgrace on the reputation of beaten biscuits, seasoned bakers did not hold back criticism.

As I explored the history and culture of Hard Jelly Cake, one of Maryland's more obscure traditions, I found a similar wellspring of passion.

Mrs. Edgar Linton's recipe in the 1966 cookbook "Maryland's Way" is one of only two recipes in my database so far. "This is an old southern Maryland receipt," wrote Linton, "popular at Christmas time. A Shady Side specialty, it keeps very well and looks festive when sliced thin."

With only recipes to go on, I couldn't really envision what the cake was meant to taste and feel like. A few years ago, my aunt from Shady Side purchased one from Elaine Catterton. Catterton is one of the few bakers carrying on the tradition, making cakes for raffle/sale around the holidays.

The wax paper wrapping and red string were clearly part of the experience of Hard Jelly Cake. The cookie-like layers were infused with the flavor of grape jelly. The cake was not like any cake I'd ever had before.

This unique dessert is another multi-layered specialty dessert hailing from a small town on the water. The similarities to Smith Island Cake end there. Hard Jelly Cake has not found a fan base far beyond the descendants and social circle of the families who popularized the cake in Shady Side a hundred and fifty years ago. Despite its rarity, the cakes are still made and sold around

Christmastime in Shady Side, and mentioning its name is sure to bring fond memories to those who are familiar with it.

Valerie Carson Watson grew up in the Annapolis area and had a network of friends and family who made Hard Jelly Cake.

She grew up knowing the cake was special. "A lot of work and love" went into baking the cakes, which were put into a cookie tin wrapped in wax paper to age for a month before being served.

"It was a Christmas tradition," she told me. "My grandmother and her sisters made hard jelly and then my mom and then me," she said. Across the marsh from Watson's family lived another Hard Jelly Cake baker, Ida "Honeybaby" Harpe, the aunt of Watson's friend Jeanne Ewald. "Jeanne's grandmother and her sister's made the hard jelly cakes as well. Jeanne's mother continued and then Jeanne and I started making them. Ida's grand-daughter makes them now too." In 2020, Jeanne and Valerie's cake-baking had to go on pause due to COVID precautions.

On the origin of the cake in Watson's social circle, she said "my older sister, Leslie thinks Hard Jelly Cakes started with the Townsend sisters. My grandmother was a Townsend from Davidsonville. Ida's son, Neil think it started with the Owings sisters. The Owings family were from Shady Side." The origin story takes a backseat to the social bonds represented by cake-making.

Online recipes for the cake turn up the tight web of the social connections of a small town like Shady Side. The comments on one blog post mention Ida "Honeybaby" Harpe by name.

It's rare that a recipe can be traced definitively to a family, but it is fairly likely that the Hard Jelly Cake originated with the Hartges and spread through their family tree and the surrounding community.

Anton Heinrich Gottlieb "Henry" Hartge left Germany along with a few of his nephews in 1832. Hartge had experience as a piano builder and that is what he did for several years in Baltimore. He originated a method of using an iron frame in his pianos. One of Hartge's employees, another German man named William Knabe, went on to become a well-known piano manufacturer in

Baltimore using this design.

Legend has it that Henry Hartge visited Shady Side to tune a piano and decided to stay, around 1845. Henry's grandson Emile Alexander Hartge turned the family woodworking business in a more regional direction and began building ships. Hartge Yacht Yard, founded in 1865, may be one of the oldest boat-yards in the country.

Hard Jelly Cake bears more than a passing resemblance to Baumkuchen, or "Tree Cake," a German Christmas specialty. That cake sometimes incorporates things like almond paste and apricot jam, and is coated in chocolate. In 19th-century Shady Side it became something simpler, and entirely unique.

It is worth noting that cakes, like most recipes, tend to be passed matrilineally. Names, on the other hand, are patrilineal. Valerie's sister Leslie Trettau said "I asked a couple of the Hartge's about the hard jelly cake and they never heard of it." It was women who shared this cake recipe with one-another. Whether it was Henry's wife Emily Tscheripe, Henry & Emily's son Fernando's German-born wife Mary Doerr, or another German woman who popularized the layered jelly cake in Shady Side, the Hartge family is just one piece in the Hard Jelly Cake story.

In a 1975 article in the Annapolis Capital Gazette, Edna Collinson (1912-1992) of Deale connected Hard Jelly Cake to the Hartge family as she prepared them with her daughter Jeannine Tucker. Ethel Andrews of Shady Side reminisced about the special cake. "It was a Shady Side [Christmas] custom to visit all of the homes," she said. "And in those homes there were tables laden with approximately 20 homemade cakes. The hard jelly cake occupied a prominent place."

A few years earlier, in 1967, a Maryland-born woman named Virginia Morris shared her recipe for Hard Jelly Cake with the Salt Lake City Deseret News. Morris' recipe contains twice the flour as Mrs. Edgar Linton's recipe. A comparable ratio appears in recipes shared online. It may be that the Maryland's Way recipe was a typo, which would certainly alter the experience of making the cake.

As a part of a military family, another Hard Jelly Cake enthusiast,

Deborah Ford, 74, lived in Germany for ten years. She visited factories to find pans like the ones she inherited and uses to make the cake. Her search came up fruitless, and the cakes in Europe failed to stoke the taste of home that Hard Jelly Cake represents. "They do many different torte cakes but they are more like a cake and only a few layers. I was disappointed. Guess it is a dying art world wide." She continued to make the cakes herself to keep the tradition alive.

Making the cake is a minefield of missteps. Lacking a way to cut the dough discs, I used a saucepan. I then realized I was in the predicament of sliding the slabs onto a pan to be baked. I'd recommend parchment paper!

There are the things only a seasoned Hard Jelly Cake-baker would know – how dark to cook the layers, just how thick to spread the jelly... and then there is the matter of taste and substitutions – each alteration a potential sacrilege.

Although the recipe in Maryland's Way called for currant jelly, by most modern accounts, a love of authentic Hard Jelly Cake requires an appreciation of grape jelly. Watson recalled that her grandmother had a grapevine in her yard. The smell and taste of Elaine Catterton's cake evoked memories of peanut butter and jelly sandwiches for me.

I made my own cake with elderberry jam because I had it on hand. But I must profess I do not have a great love of grape jelly. "Sorry," Valerie Watson said, "but that's all the ladies used when making their cakes."

I was happy with my results, but a lot depends on the flavor of the jelly.

I may purchase another Hard Jelly Cake if I have the opportunity, but I doubt I'll frequently make my inauthentic non-grape version. Hard Jelly Cake is, after all, someone else's tradition. I have some of my own.

On Christmas Eve's Day 2020, we got a car and drove around delivering my Vanilla Butternut Cakes to family and friends.

After leaving a pound cake with my aunt in Shady Side, I stopped to view the Hartge cemetery. Like many small family cemeteries, it sits nearly in someone's backyard. The old tombstones poke out at different angles, sinking into the marshy earth, with the West River in the background. The Hartge Yacht Yard still operates on the other side of the river.

We went on our way and I spent the day dropping little gold cake boxes on porches, stoops and mailboxes, occasionally exchanging a smile or a text message with people I missed dearly. Loving traditions will always morph and change to match our resources. Baumkuchen became Hard Jelly Cake.

"I realized once I left Shady Side that no place out of our area knew about [Hard Jelly Cakes]," said Deborah Ford. She left the area in 1968, bringing the cake tradition along. "That was the one home memory I kept alive for many years no matter where we were stationed. I sure miss the quiet little village on the Chesapeake Bay." ❀

Hard Jelly Cake

1 Cup shortening	.5 Teaspoon salt
1 Cup sugar	.5 Teaspoon nutmeg
1 egg	.5 Cup milk
3.5 Cup flour	1.5 glass red currant jelly
2.5 Teaspoon baking powder	[about 3 fl oz]

Cream together the shortening, sugar and egg. Sift dry ingredients and add alternately with milk to creamed mixture. Chill dough. Take a small piece of chilled dough and roll until thin. Select the top of a cooking pot or a small plate of the size desired and, after dough is rolled, place it on top and, using a pie crimper or a knife, cut a circle of dough the shape of guide. Using two spatulas, slip one under each side of circle and carefully lift it onto greased cookie sheet. A large cookie sheet holds three 7" circles. Bake at 350° for 8 to 10 minutes.

When browned slightly, remove from oven, place one layer on cake plate, spread with jelly, put another warm layer on top, spread with jelly, and continue in this manner until you have a jelly layer cake with about 10 to 14 layers. To make a pretty cake, before baking the last layer, sprinkle it with red colored sugar crystals. Also, it may be sprinkled with powdered sugar after baking. Makes 2 cakes, 7" in diameter or 10 to 12 layers.

Recipe adapted from "Maryland's Way: The Hammond-Harwood House Cookbook"

Hard Jelly Cake

Our Daily Bread

Our Church

Centenary United Methodist
Shady Side, Maryland

Give thanks to God for each day's precious gift
Of varied food, with which our tastes we please;
For those who grow and those who process it,
And those who concoct books of recipes.

But food can often be quite ill prepared,
And there is little nourishment in books;
Fine recipes demand a loving touch:
So pause a while and praise God for good cooks.

HARD JELLY CAKE

Miss Leslie Avery *

7 c. flour
5 t. baking powder
nutmeg
1 c. white sugar
1 c. brown sugar
1½ c. Crisco

½ c. butter
2 eggs
1 c. milk
vanilla
jelly

Sift together the flour and baking powder. Add
nutmeg, sugar, Crisco and butter and beat well.
Add milk and vanilla to beaten eggs and add to
creamed flour, sugar, and Crisco mixture. This
will make 28-9" layers. We prefer the 12 layer
cakes. Roll out very thin on the bottom of
greased and floured cake pans. Bake until light
brown in moderate oven. Layers can be stored
in dry place and jellied as needed, if desired.

Brown Stone Front, Mrs. Byron S. Dorsey

Posted on December 11, 2021

Mrs. Brown, the first-nameless protagonist of playwright Chandos Fulton's 1873 novelette, responds witheringly to the news that a friend's daughter has wed a man of modest means. "It was a love-match, I suppose," her friend Mrs. Campbell told her, and Mrs. Brown "did not deign a reply."

As the plot of Fulton's novel unfolds, Mrs. Brown meddles in her own daughter Adele's romantic life, breaking off a would-be "love-match," to fix Adele up with a wealthier suitor. Adele's marriage to the moneyed fellow is an unhappy one, and a scandal breaks out when people incorrectly suspect Adele of having an affair with another man. It turns out that Adele was just lonely, and when Adele's cold-but-wealthy husband Mr. Dick comes to understand this, he becomes an ideal husband on command. Adele Brown and her ambitious busybody mother both get a happy ending. The original love-match man who broke Adele's heart due to Mrs. Brown's scheming in Chapter Four is never mentioned again.

Mrs. Brown's desire for Adele to marry a wealthy man is symbolized by a status-symbol that serves as the book's title: "A Brown Stone Front."

Newspapers in New York City had been advertising "brown stone front" buildings for sale and rent since the 1840s. Other cities followed suit, and a "brown stone front" remained an attractive selling point in real-estate for the better part of the following century.

What was originally a cheaper and easier-cut alternative to marble and limestone became synonymous with success in America.

According to Charles Lockwood in his 1972 book, "Bricks ₹ Brownstone: The New York Row House, 1783-1929 An Architectural ₹ Social History": "In the 1840s and early 1850s, New Yorkers and visitors to the city admired the 'unostentatious

42   Brown Stone Front

magnificence' and 'refinement' of its brownstone-front mansions and row houses, and within several years nearly all of New York's large row houses were built with the fashionable brownstone front."

While New York's association with brownstone buildings remains famous to this day, the material was used throughout the eastern seaboard and in New Orleans. Quarries in Portland, Connecticut and Little Falls, New Jersey provided much of the material which can be found on buildings in Baltimore neighborhoods like Mount Vernon and Bolton Hill.

The somewhat awkward and particular name "brown stone front" refers to the fact that the soft stone served only as a façade, attached to the front of buildings made of brick.

When the sandstone known as "brownstone" is first cut, it has more of a pink color. The hematite iron ore quickly oxidizes and matures into the brown color which inspired 19th-century bakers to name a chocolate cake in honor of the coveted brownstone-veneered buildings.

What exactly defines this cake is a little vague. A dense, pound-cake-like texture is fairly common, although some recipes are more leavened. With the recipe I used, the cake was so heavy and dense that the icing was squished out from between the layers.

The filling is sometimes an egg-white icing, like in my recipe. Some call for a filling of jelly or chopped nuts.

A caramel icing between layers is a popular version that makes sense aesthetically and flavor-wise. In the 1904 "Maryland Cook Book," 'Miss Page' contributed a recipe entitled "Chocolate Cake (Brownstone Front)." That recipe states that the cake "may be filled with either a white filling or caramel—caramel preferred." If I make a Brown Stone Front cake again, I will take the hint.

Cinnamon, cloves, raisins, and coffee are additions in various other recipes. Like many of the named cakes that made the rounds in the 1800s, Brown Stone Front Cake is more about the idea of a cake than about a specific expectation.

This recipe was contributed to "Choice Maryland Cookery" by Mrs. B. S. Dorsey, in 1902. Byron S. Dorsey was a prominent merchant of farm equipment in Mt. Airy, Carroll County near where "Choice Maryland Cookery" was published. His wife's name was Martha, but all of the census and findagrave information I found about her is wildly conflicting.

Another research obstacle was figuring out what Mrs. Dorsey meant by "half cake of chocolate." Luckily this one wasn't a dead end. An 1896 cookbook from Seattle had a recipe that called for "1/2 cake of chocolate (1/4 lb)." A second source confirmed this standard, and so I used 1/4 pound of chocolate. Unexpected density aside, this was a pretty good cake and a little slice went a long way.

I had entertained the possibility that "Brown Stone Front" cake could be named more directly for Chandos Fulton's novelette. It wouldn't be unheard of. A decade or two after the Brown Stone Front Cake entered the scene, Owen Wister's 1906 novel "Lady Baltimore" would create a craze for that titular cake.

This possibility was laid to rest when I looked into the cultural impact of Fulton's story. It was panned by critics. In scathing Victorian language, the Brooklyn Review called the story "a pleasantish little outline sketch... illustrative of the rather trite subject of marrying for money... It involves no original studies either of character or society," the review went on, and commenting on the forced and unromantic happy ending the reviewer said, "a defiance of the traditional moralities regarding the end of mercenary marriages... gives the book its one soupçon of originality."

The Chicago Weekly Post was more forthright: "One had better pay 75¢ to avoid reading it, than the same sum in purchase of the book."

Brown Stone Front cake was somewhat more enduring, if not as permanent a fixture as the buildings that the cake celebrates. ✻

Brown Stone Front

Two cups sugar, one cup butter, one cup milk, six eggs,
four cups flour, four teaspoons of yeast powder or Royal
baking powder. Mix half cake chocolate in a little hot
water until perfectly smooth, stir in one and one-half
cups of scalding milk. Beat yolks of two eggs, two cups
sugar together, add one teaspoon of vanilla, pour on
hot milk and chocolate and let cool, then mix. Use white
icing between layers.
MRS. B. S. DORSEY

Recipe from "Choice Maryland Cookery", Printed at the Caroll Record Office, 1902

*The Garrett-Jacobs Mansion in Mount Vernon, built in 1853, is one of Baltimore's grandest
brownstone-fronted buildings. Library of Congress photo.*

Hoppin John for New Year's

Posted on December 31, 2019

The 1958 "Historical Cookbook of the American Negro," by the National Council of Negro Women, opens with a photograph of Sojourner Truth and Abraham Lincoln, opposite recipes for the first of January: "Emancipation Proclamation Breakfast Cake" from Newark, New Jersey and "Western Beef Steak" from Denver. "The Emancipation Proclamation New Years' Day, 1863, is celebrated in all parts of the United States. The Council recipes... have been taken from the oldest files of Negro families," the book explains below the recipes.

The subsequent recipe is for "Southern Hopping John." No further explanations were needed for what this recipe meant and where it came from. The caption instead points out the similarity to another recipe in the book, for Haitian "Plate National," a dish of rice and beans enjoyed in Haiti, where Independence Day is January 1st. The book also includes a rice and beans recipe from Ghana. Together, the recipes imply a powerful message about food and heritage.

Oral histories given by local residents to the St. Mary's College Slackwater Center describe New Year's traditions in Southern Maryland throughout the 20th century to the present day.

Residents of the Black farming communities there described New Year's as a kind of end to a season of celebration and relaxation. Philip H. Scriber, Sr. fondly recalled that "from Christmas to New Year no one did any work. They spent the whole holiday socializing. They made homemade cakes and root beer. In those days you didn't have the money, but you had the love."

Esther Smith described men in St. Mary's County trying to be the first to cross into others' households for good luck, "going to people's houses first thing in the morning on New Year's Day." Smith also described the custom of eating black-eyed peas and hogs' heads for New Year's. "Safeway stores and all... they have it ready for that day."

South Carolina-born Professor Jefferey Coleman explained that "collard greens meant, you know, money and prosperity and the black-eyed peas meant change."

In "Fighting Old Nep: The Foodways of Enslaved Afro-Marylanders 1634-1864," historian Michael Twitty wrote of his childhood memories of eating black-eyed peas on New Year's Day, as well as "putting them in everyone's wallet or pocketbook so that they would have money for the entire year." Twitty traced black-eyed peas' presence in Maryland to the 1750s.

Famed chef and Virginia native Edna Lewis described their use in her second book, "The Taste of Country Cooking": "They were not planted in the garden but were planted by farmers as a green manure crop. Before the sowing of wheat, when in full foliage, they were chopped into the soil. A week before, everyone was welcome to gather the green pods before the crop was chopped under" in the late summer and fall. Lewis mentioned the beans' African origin, noting that the legume was "always an exponent of agriculture" for its nitrogen and soil-building qualities.

Despite the long-standing presence of black-eyed peas in Maryland and Virginia, old Maryland recipes for Hoppin' John almost all come from South Carolina, where the dish probably originated. A 1904 recipe in a boxed set of "Colonial Cook Cards" is attributed to the "Rose family" of Charleston. Reverend Hunter-Wyatt Brown, Jr., who was raised in Baltimore, contributed a recipe to the 1954 "Personal Recipes compiled by the Esther Circle St. Timothy's Church" of Catonsville cookbook. Wyatt-Brown was born in North Carolina but entitled his recipe "Hoppin' John (Old South Carolina)." The recipe that Rachel adapted was contributed by Greenville, South Carolina-born Louise Kelly to the 1975 community cookbook "300 Years of Black Cooking in St. Mary's County."

With West African-by-way-of-South Carolina origins, the deep-rooted tradition has been adopted by Marylanders of all races. No one wants to forego good luck on New Years' Day! ✱

Hoppin' John for New Year's

.5 Lb salt pork   1 small onion, chopped, optional
2 Cups water   salt to taste
1 Lb black-eyed peas   pepper to taste
1 Cup rice   1 Tablespoon sugar (optional)

  Put the salt pork in the water and let it simmer until it is tender. Wash and pick over the peas. You can soak them overnight if you wish. Add the peas to the meat, and cook until tender, but don't let them go dry. Set aside. Cook rice as usual, but cook so it is dry. Slowly stir the rice into the peas. Add the onion if you want, salt, pepper, and sugar if you like. Simmer to gravy-like thickness.

Recipe from "300 Years of Black Cooking in St. Mary's County Maryland," Citizens for Progress, 1975

300 years
of
Black Cooking
In
St. Mary's County
Maryland

H. Franklyn Hall's "Crab Cakes"

Posted on October 31, 2020

"Men become cooks because they have a love for the calling," wrote Harry Franklyn Hall in "Good Housekeeping" in 1903. The article he wrote described the passion and career progression of men (specifically) in the food industry and the stress one must endure as he gains skills and experience to become "an eighth-degree cook." Despite the annoying implication that only men can "excel in the art of cooking" and "reach its loftiest height," the article details the many techniques Hall personally mastered in the rise from dishwasher to famed chef. Together with the listing of his places of employment in his 1901 book "300 Ways to Cook and Serve Shellfish," it is closest thing we have to a career autobiography of Hall.

Hall was one of the famed Black caterers working in posh hotels at the turn of the 20th century. Although Philadelphia had a hotel and seafood culture to rival Baltimore's, it doesn't appear to have been as much a point of pride for the city and its press. At least in the digitized documents I have access to, H. Franklyn Hall's name isn't mentioned in the papers as much as his Baltimore contemporaries like John R. Young.

Hall was born in D.C. on December 22, 1853. Both of his parents were born in Maryland. In 1872 he married Georgia Brown, also from D.C. In 1900, they were living in Philadelphia where he was working as a chef. In 1910, he is listed as a restaurant "proprietor." Georgia died in 1927, and in 1930, Hall was lodging with a family at 5609 Wyalusing Avenue with no occupation listed. He died of an aneurysm on December 14th, 1935. His address at the time was 2048 Pemberton St. The informant on his death certificate was a Madelyn P. McPherson of New York City.

Unfortunately, Hall's financial woes are one of the few remnants of his life that ended up documented. In "300 Ways to Cook and Serve Shellfish," he made pleas for money. His name sometimes appeared in newspapers in connection with his money troubles.

Still, he must have had some degree of celebrity in his lifetime. His most known chef position was at the Boothby Hotel, which seems to have been highly regarded. Hall's claim in his book's preface that Boothby had "the generally acknowledged largest and finest oyster and shell fish department in the world" was at least somewhat backed up by the press, which frequently mentioned the business and its owners' other ventures. Newspapers in Accomac County Virginia also frequently mentioned employees of the Boothby. One of the hotel managers, D.J. Whealton, owned a huge oyster bed in Chincoteague.

In 1904, Hall used his prestige to promote a kitchen appliance that he invented "to save labor in hotels, hospitals and restaurants." Advertisements show a variety of attachments for whipping eggs, mashing potatoes, and sifting flour.

As far as I can tell, the "Hall Kitchen King," as it was known, was manufactured into the 1920s. It is possible that Hall sold or lost the rights to his machine as his name is not mentioned in trade publications after 1904. In the 1910 "Philadelphia Colored Directory" he took out an ad naming himself as the inventor of the device, called "the greatest invention of the age."

"300 Ways to Cook and Serve Shellfish" was successful enough that Hall wrote another book, "How to Make and Serve 100 Choice Broths and Soups" in 1903. That book has unfortunately not made it into the public domain yet although there are copies in library collections.

I hope to access the soup book one day and see if Hall shared any more information about his career (or even his finances.)

Maryland is well represented in "300 Ways to Cook and Serve Shellfish" which contains well over a dozen dishes named for Maryland or Baltimore. The recipe for "Lobster Claws Á La Maryland" may be inspired by Maryland Fried Chicken. The claws are battered and fried, served with bacon, a cream sauce, and "fried diamond or crescent shaped hominy" fritters.

Hall included recipes for soft shell crab sandwiches served essentially as they're eaten today – on white bread with tartar sauce and lettuce. Another very contemporary-seeming sandwich recipe calls for thinly sliced chicken breast, served with crab meat and lettuce on bread.

The instructions on picking hard crabs is even more opaque than the recipes are:

"After the crab has thoroughly cooled simply cut the body in half and crack the claws, pick out all of the firm white meat and fat; throw everything else away."

One of the unique and notable things about "300 Ways to Cook and Serve Shellfish" is that it contains an entire section on Oyster Crabs, with sixteen recipes for the tiny parasitic crabs. I have recipes in my collection that mention oyster crabs, which were sometimes served atop soup, but they rarely merit more than a mention. With the high volume of oysters sold at Boothby, Hall was apparently able to serve them in salads, timbales, on toasts, and in omelets with "twenty-five to forty live oyster crabs for every portion." The tiny crabs within the omelet were to be boiled and served in a cream sauce, on a plate garnished with additional oyster crabs and chopped parsley. It must have been quite a presentation.

I mentioned Hall's Crab Cake recipe in my "History of Crab Cakes". This recipe is essentially a seafood pancake made with crab.

There are recipes for crab cakes as we now know them that pre-date Hall's book, but there is no reason that Hall would be reading cookbooks aimed at housewives. Hall's own book, though ostensibly directed at "the lady of the house", is arranged similarly to Delmonico chef Charles Ranhofer's epic 1893 cookbook, "The Epicurean" which had a chef audience in mind. Many of the recipes reference a cascade of other recipes in the book, leaving the reader flipping around through the book to follow the steps in order.

H. Fryankln Hall is another Black chef whose contribution to our dining culture should be recognized. His "Crab Cakes" bear too little similarity to modern crab cakes to bother getting riled up about authenticity. They stand on their own merit. Despite Hall's Philadelphia citizenship, paired with some eggs and seasonal vegetables this felt like a very Maryland breakfast. ❅

Treasurer and Manager
Chelsea Restaurant Company, Inc.
1308 Sansom Street
Philadelphia

H. FRANKLYN HALL

AUTHOR and INVENTOR
OF THE
"KITCHEN KING"

The Greatest Invention of the Age.

An Authority on all Cuisine and Culinary matters.

The Hall Kitchen King Machine

PATENTED

Saves labor and never quits the job. It is cheaper than hand labor and saves time also. Put it in your hotel now and be ready for the rush.

King of Machines for Kitchen Use. A well deserved title for these reasons:

1st—The valuable time of the chef is saved by this machine owing to its adaptability in every use in the preparation of food stuffs. It does not have to be watched the same as the help, but will perform its duties carefully, cleanly and in a far more satisfactory manner than by hand. To do this one just has to learn as he will know the work will be done properly and on time.

2nd—It will increase the quantity of your food products 33 1-3 per cent over hand work, thus making a tremendous saving.

3rd—You will require less help in your kitchen. Let the machine do the work, and it will pay for itself with six months.

4th—It never gives out or tires.

5th—Will prepare a meal for 500 persons as quickly as it is being run for hand, or prepare same meal for 50 persons.

6th—It is so invaluable for the Bakers' department as it is for kitchen purposes.

7th—There is no machine made that is a competitor to this line, and if is hard to see how a first class or any other kitchen can be without it and pretend to be economical.

8th—It is made for endurance. Simple in construction, any one can run it. PRICE so reasonable that people interested will be able to have one or more.

REQUIRES 18 IN. x 24 IN. FLOOR SPACE AND IS 60 IN. HIGH.

Capacity 1 to 40 quarts.

This Machine Will Do Almost Any Work Now Done by Hand

It will mash one bushel of potatoes in four minutes and produce them as light as sponge cake and increases one-third in bulk.

It will make **Mayonnaise Dressing,** one pint or four gallons in six minutes.

Whip Egg, white or yolks. Will produce egg whites, three for one.

Sieve Flour, meal and sugar. One barrel of flour in four minutes.

It **Will Pass** all kinds of sauces, jellies and fruits through a sieve. In passing fruits it will leave only dry pulp without a particle of waste. It will pass all kinds of soups and purees.

In time and labor saved and increased production of food, this machine will pay for itself in a very short time.

This machine will **make the finest butter** without the least trouble or waste of time. One noted chef says: "It will do most everything except talk".

All good things have imitators. We manufacture under our patents the best machine on the market. **Infringements by manufacturers and users will henceforth be prosecuted.**

Ask Your Jobber for Prices and Booklet or Send to

THE HALL KITCHEN KING CO. 1335 Arch St., Philadelphia, Pa.

Crab Cakes, Butter Sauce

Make a stiff, rich cake, batter thin, mix in enough crab meat to make stiff. Cook on grid-iron or in a smooth bottom fry pan same as griddle or pan cakes; serve with drawn butter for breakfast or lunch.

Recipe from 300 Ways to Cook and Serve Shellfish H. Franklyn Hall, 1901

Beef Roulades, Edyth Malin

Posted on June 4, 2023

The Dakota Cheese Company was flying high in 1983. With 11.5 million in sales of mozzarella and provolone, the 12-year-old company was expected to continue growing. Dakota Cheese president James Dee credited his government contracts for his company's success. That success was enabling expansion into private markets. Dee expected Dakota Cheese to score a big contract with "a major chain of pizza parlors" soon.

Five years later, success gave way to disgrace. Farmers stopped delivering milk. Dee was forced to sell off his company's assets to Associated Milk Producers Inc. No self-respecting pizza parlor would be associated with Dakota Cheese. Not after they'd been accused of defrauding the government.

The 1988 indictment claimed that by using calcium caseinate as an ingredient in the cheese purchased for school lunch contracts, Dakota Cheese had misled the government and violated the FDA cheese regulations.

A lab near Philadelphia completed an analysis of the cheese. They declared the mozzarella to be "phony."

The company was done for.

But the Philadelphia scientists were just getting started. The analysis had them inspired. Perhaps mozzarella cheese could be altered within the confines of FDA law. Perhaps it could be improved upon, made lower fat, without sacrificing taste and texture. The lab took on the name "The Mozarella Group."

By 1994, the scientists were homing in on new ways to make pizza and string cheese lower-fat, for the health of dieters and schoolchildren alike.

"It's easy to make low-fat cheese," the lead scientist explained. "The problem is texture." Mozzarella was of particular interest. "Everyone [else] was working on cheddar," she said.

Her name was Edyth Malin. She was born in 1926 in Fitchburg,

Massachussetts to Joseph and Marie Lasky. In 1947, she married Morton V. Malin, who she met while attending Vanderbilt University.

After marrying, the Malins lived in Chillum, Maryland, and later, Rockville and Silver Spring. And so, in 1980, Edyth contributed two recipes to "Treasures from our Tables," a cookbook compiled by the Sisterhood of the Temple Shalom in Chevy Chase.

There is nothing about Edyth's recipes for Cornish Hens and Beef Roulades that would give you any indication that she would develop a groundbreaking method for reducing the fat content from cheeses. Her 2018 obituary mentioned the accomplishment and the fact that she was a member and volunteer for the Association for Women In Science (AWIS).

The mozzarella group wasn't done bringing phony cheesemongers to justice. In the early 1990s, they analyzed some imported buffalo mozzarella, finding it contained only traces of buffalo milk. The importers learned what the Dakota Cheese company had learned: you don't want to go up against the Mozzarella Group. ✳

Beef Roulades

1 Lb beef sliced thin	garlic powder to taste
1 Cup soft breadcrumbs	melted butter
.25 to .5 Cup fresh or canned mush-room stems & pieces	1Lb fresh mushroom caps
salt to taste	1 Cup dry red wine
pepper to taste	vegetable oil
.5 to .75c Cup shredded Parmesan	Accent
.5 Cup minced parsley, fresh or frozen	

Use thin slices of round steak usually called braciales. Figure on 1 slice per person for men and a half slice for women. These slices should be 6 to 8 inches wide and about 10 to 12 inches long. Cut each slice in half crosswise. Pound with a wooden mallet until absolutely tender and quite thin. Prepare the stuffing with the bread crumbs, Parmesan cheese, parsley and mushroom stems and pieces, with salt, pepper and garlic powder to taste. Add just enough butter to hold together. Place 1 tablespoon of filling on each piece of meat, roll and fasten with skewer or tie. Brown the mushroom caps in half butter and half oil in a skillet. Remove and set aside. Brown rolls in same skillet, season with salt, pepper and Accent. Return mushrooms to pan, add wine, cover and simmer 30 to 45 minutes until meat is tender. Remove skewers and serve. If there is too much juice, remove rolls and simmer juice down. Serve over rolls. Serves 4 to 6.

Recipe from Treasures From our Tables, Sisterhood of Temple Shalom, Chevy Chase, 1980

Snowball Flavorings, 1912

Posted on August 26, 2018

Of all the casualties of the car-centric highway age of Baltimore, perhaps the reduction in neighborhood snowball stands looms the largest on sweaty summer strolls through town. The ice cream trucks are great but... just not the same.

When in 1977 the Baltimore Sun ran one of their many annual celebrations of the beloved summer treat, they estimated "perhaps 1000" snowball stands operating in the city – about one for every 822 people.

Although the 2012 SnoBaltimore map never claimed to be comprehensive – snowball stands these days are often ephemeral or hard to pin down – the number was closer to one snowball stand for every 4500 residents (locations in the county included due to my laziness.)

Aside from the lack of foot traffic necessary to do a bustling streetside trade in snowballs, sporadic health-code enforcements may have dampened business a bit. There were at least four stands within a square block of 25th and Greenmount, the Sun reported in 1977, and it was "a very profitable business."

These days, snowballs may generate less profit, but certainly no less enthusiasm. The 1977 article continued a long tradition of venerating the snowball as a part of Baltimore summers. A search through the archive will confirm that at least the tradition of *writing* about snowballs is alive and well.

Their origin has been speculated to have been a byproduct of the ice-wagon trade, but snowballs were a business onto their own by the late 1800s. Newspapers advertised supplies – shavers and flavorings (bring your own bottle).

Even in Frederick, the News reported that "on a very warm evening [in 1895] the demand for snow-balls is quite brisk." Young boys would scrape ice from a large block, add a "dash or two of some variety of syrup" and sell it for a penny. The "ambitious youngsters" did "thriving business" on a bustling

Market Street full of strolling shoppers, U.S. Cavalrymen, and occasional unruly horses.

By 1932, the Afro-American referred to Snowballs as "those Baltimore Delicacies," plied in sheds, "cubby holes between two houses," or "other sort[s] of arrangements." They noted that unemployment was driving more and more men into the business of peddling summer refreshments.

And indeed, snowballs did provide another avenue for Black Baltimore citizens to make a living in a segregated city. A 1938 story about grocer William A Fitzgerald, of Harlem Park, ran with the headline that he got his start in business selling snowballs and peanuts. Originally started in defiance of a grocer who'd called the police on an elderly woman selling snowballs, Fitzgerald's own business grew into a store that sold "almost anything imaginable," and employed local youth.

Immigrants like Reuben Platt also found a living in snowballs. Born to a Jewish Lithuanian family in 1909, it is an interesting but not unlikely coincidence that Platt's boyhood neighbor was an ice wagon laborer. When Platt was laid off from a warehouse job in 1959, he went into business selling snowballs, and was still in business when the Sun profiled him in 1971. He offered many insights into the business. People don't buy snowballs until it gets really hot. Heat waves rarely lasted longer than ten days. Chocolate was the best selling flavor, followed by cherry, root-beer, grape, sky-lite (raspberry-vanilla), spearmint, kola, and lemon.

That last bit may come as a slight surprise to modern snowball aficionados. Egg custard has become the iconic popular favorite, but most snowball coverage through the years corroborated Platt. The 1977 Sun story claimed, "if there is such a thing as the 'Baltimore snowball,' it would be the chocolate flavored variety, topped with marshmallow."

I can't pinpoint when exactly egg custard gained favor. Nor am I certain when marshmallow became a standard offering. Perhaps those are stories for another day.

Tastes change, regardless. In 1949, when the Sun discussed snowballs from the perspective of a confused "Virginian traveling through Maryland," strawberry was apparently the "unrivaled favorite." Marshmallow cream was then an "imaginative" embellishment mentioned along with crushed fruit or cherries.

"Most snowball dealers find it economical to buy concentrated extracts and make their own flavors by adding sugar and water," the article wrote. As a long-standing commercially produced item, few recipes exist. I never expected to be writing this. In 1912, a reader wrote to the Sun demanding recipes for "several kinds of snowball flavoring" and the newspaper obliged. Whether these formulas have any kind of authenticity is highly questionable.

Nonetheless, I took a shot at the chocolate and raspberry syrups.

Some friends had the brilliant idea of having a snowball syrup party, affording me the perfect opportunity to test these out (plus taste a dozen innovative flavors made by more creative people.) At around $75 a week to rent a Koldkiss machine, this ought to become a Baltimore party fad. We could all have a chance to come up with a flavor to give chocolate, egg custard, strawberry or even sky-lite a run for their money. ❀

Snowball Flavorings

Chocolate – Take 8 ounces of chocolate, 1 quart of water and 4 pounds of white sugar. Mix the chocolate in water and stir thoroughly over a slow fire. Strain and add the sugar.

Strawberry – Wash the fruit well, then put on the stove in a saucepan without adding any more water. Cover with a lid and let the berries come to a boil, but do not boil them. Stir occasionally. When well heated mash the fruit well with a wooden potato masher then strain through a fine sieve, being careful to get every drop of substance from the fruit. Sweeten the juice with sugar to taste, ad a few drops of lemon juice, put back on the stove and cook until it thicken, stirring occasionally. This can be used for blackberries, strawberries and raspberries.

Vanilla (note the large quantities, suggesting this may have been more popular):

Take 14 pounds of white sugar and add 1 gallon of water. Dissolve with the aid of gentle heat and when cold add 2 ounces of extract of vanilla.

Recipes from the Baltimore Evening Sun, July 12, 1912

Hokey-Pokey

"I suppose they gave it that name because it isn't real, good, genuine ice-cream—just sort of a sham. You know, a 'hocus-pocus' is another word for a 'hoax,' or trick. So hokey-pokey ice-cream is a cheat. It's cold and tastes sweet, but it isn't good, clean wholesome food." – Modern Physiology Hygiene and Health primer, 1921

Summer always causes me to revisit the storied history of Baltimore snowballs. As I have mentioned, the snowball endured many waves of health code threats. Luckily, nostalgia won out and snowballs have become something of a sacred cow when it comes to licensing crackdowns.

At the turn of the 20th century, there was an also-ran summer confection that didn't fare quite as well.

Hokey-pokey first appeared on the streets of London in the mid-1800s, sold by Italian vendors. The name is believed to be a variant of "hocus pocus," or -some say- derived from vendors calling out "ecco un poco": "here's a little." Unless that is a popular street-vendor call in Italy, I'm skeptical.

Hokey-pokey quickly made its way to New York, to beach towns like Long Branch New Jersey, and eventually to Baltimore.

For something so wildly popular, very few people ever knew just what hokey-pokey actually was. A traveler from Buffalo New York visiting London described a hokey-pokey vendor "taking from an ice-cream freezer a little square of something that looked like a slice of white castile soap" in 1879. The Hamlin, Kansas News Gleaner claimed in 1880 that "the hokey-pokey is made largely of corn starch and milk." In 1889, the Hampshire Telegraph in England wrote that "it is difficult to say, nowadays, what is 'hokey-pokey' and what it is not."

Even some would-be vendors were themselves not entirely sure. A 1902 classified ad in the Baltimore Sun read: "WANTED—A Man Who Understands How to Make Hokey-Pokey Ice-Cream."

Few recipes for hokey-pokey exist, but they tend to contain varying quantities of milk, sugar, eggs, gelatin and/or cornstarch. These are all acceptable dessert ingredients, but hokey-pokey got a bad reputation. A syndicated column in 1891 declared that love is not like ice cream – it is like hokey-pokey ice cream:

"You lay down your penny; you demand your square. It's given to you on a piece of brown paper; it looks fascinating... At first it is delightful. The second mouthful is cool, but suggestive of oleomargarine; the third is waxy and sticky; and then you take the last with a wry face and are disgusted for buying it; feel that it has upset your heart[/stomach] and that you never want any more again."

The Milwaukee Weekly Wisconsin described the flavor of hokey-pokey in 1890 as "a mingled taste of paregoric, petroleum and tallow." They did concede that it was a bargain at 2 cents a bar.

When the newspapers weren't looking down on the quality of hokey-pokey, they were wringing their hands over its safety. With an unsettling dose of anti-Italian sentiment, hokey-pokey ice cream was declared to be a danger to children.

Of course, it was a dangerous time for food in general. Ice cream in particular was often suspected to be a source of deadly food poisoning.

In 1904, several children's deaths were attributed to hokey-pokey in New York. The Baltimore Sun picked up one story of a Harlem girl who died after eating three hokey-pokey ice cream sandwiches. A child in Manhattan died from "some kind of poison," which the Brooklyn Daily Eagle reported was "presumably" from hokey-pokey, which the boy had been fond of. The persistence of this summer treat was under threat of being banished from cities.

Ultimately, it was the ice cream lobby who encouraged a crackdown. When the Maryland Ice-Cream Manufacturers Association met at the Emerson in 1913, they declared that they only intended to "raise the ice cream standard," not to drive the hokey-pokey men out of business. Nonetheless, health commissioners were asked to help "exterminate" hokey-pokey carts, and they soon began to fade from memory in Baltimore.

In 1921, Hokey-Pokey was still apparently enough of a menace elsewhere to receive lengthy censure in "The Play-House," a children's schoolbook designed to teach about hygiene and health. The book's author, Mary S. Haviland, was the research secretary of the National Child Welfare Association. She wrote the book in the form of a story with lengthy dialogue where children improbably lecture one-another about the finer points of safety and food purity. In addition to learning to avoid poison ivy, to keep gasoline away from open flame, and to regularly brush their teeth, schoolchildren were warned to avoid the sweet allure of hokey-pokey.

While stating the apparently foregone conclusion that "the hokey-pokey men are usually dirty," the book explained the concept of the invisible germs to be found within the ice cream itself.

In truth, hokey-pokey never went away. While street vendors were no longer likely to manufacture the cheap ice cream in their homes, that practice was bound to die off anyway. In the early 1900s, Baltimore already had at least two factories that manufactured hokey-pokey. In the hands of corporations, hokey-pokey took other forms, including one popularized by the original hokey-pokey vendors: the ice cream sandwich. The hokey-pokey name lent itself to a popular song. Men who pushed carts to pick up trash for the city were later referred to as "hokey pokey men."

In 1966, brothers James and Elmer Mason reminisced in the Baltimore Sun about their hokey-pokey selling days, when they had to arrive by 8am to "Mr. Winn's" factory at Sarah Ann & Pearl Streets. Each day, the brothers would sell 100-200 hokey-pokey blocks for a penny apiece around Lexington Market, among a sea of pushcarts. Other vendors included the "white-aproned oystermen," banana carts, and vendors selling steamed and fried crabs. Organ-grinders would send monkeys up the drainpipes of apartment buildings to collect pennies from people who enjoyed their organ music. Like the hokey-pokey men, these 'hurdy-gurdy men' were considered "a sure sign of spring."

Spring becomes summer, which ends all too soon. In October of 1906, an anonymous poet used Baltimore's street-vendor culture to note the passing of seasons:

"The hokey-pokey man has fled,
The soda flows no more;
But the roasted-chestnut man is here—
Let the winds of autumn roar!"❀

Hokey-Pokey

"Dissolve three ounces of corn starch in one quart of milk, also soak two ounces of gelatin in a little milk or water. Place three quarts of milk and one pound and twelve ounces of sugar in a tin or porcelain-lined pan, set on the fire until boiling, then pout it over the dissolved starch and gelatin, set on the fire again and bring to a good boil, stirring constantly with the egg beater, then add one can of condensed milk, strain, cool and freeze. Flavor at will."

Recipe from "The Dispenser's Formulary, Or, Soda Water Guide," D.O. Haynes, 1915

Note: I chose a recipe with no eggs because I figured it would be closer the cheaper quality hokey-pokey. I used cherry flavoring but didn't have any food coloring.

Ambrosia & Nectar, Annunciation Greek Orthodox Cathedral

Posted on April 14, 2023

Evening Sun food columnist Virginia Roeder generally knew what she was talking about. In 1962 she announced that "a new cookbook star has appeared on the Maryland culinary horizon."

The book she was writing about would go on to earn a time-tested place on many Baltimore kitchen bookshelves. My next-door neighbors have a copy. A former coworker told me that she's "seen it on [her] godmother's shelf, so it must be good!" My own copy was donated to me from the cookbook collection of the late Dr. Patricia Smith. The book is well-used, its cover fallen off and held on with a ribbon. Opening it is like opening a gift.

The book in question, "Ambrosia & Nectar," was compiled by the Annunciation Greek Orthodox Community, and as far as I know, it was the first cookbook representation of Baltimore's Greek community, one of the largest Greek communities in the United States.

Greek immigration to Baltimore gained steam in the years between 1930 and 1950, and families moved to a neighborhood in Highlandtown known as "the Hill."

In 1975, the Baltimore Sun covered a story about a road in "Greektown, which is Baltimorese for that part of Highlandtown beyond what everyone calls 'the underpass.'"

Citizens took pride in the moniker. "The majority of people around here are Greek. They speak Greek. The main church is the Greek church. Most of the businessmen are Greeks. Whether we call it that or not, this is Greektown," said Jimmy Hajimihalis in 1979. "So we decided to call it what everybody knows it is."

The Greek Orthodox Cathedral of the Annunciation served Baltimore's Greek community since 1906, before families began settling in Highlandtown. The iconic Cathedral stands across town at the intersection of Preston and Cathedral Streets. The building was constructed to serve a Protestant congregation in 1888. Annunciation services were moved there in 1937. Each year, the church holds a Greek festival in October. 2023 will be the 50th anniversary of the festival.

"Ambrosia & Nectar's" success was followed up a decade after its publication, with 1972's "The Best of Greek Cookery." That book took the recipes and updated them, elaborated on the instructions, or switched to ingredients that were more readily available. As far as I can tell, the original remains the favorite.

Rather than listing recipe contributors' names alongside their recipes, the cookbook committee is listed at the front of the book only. Mrs. Konstantine J. Prevas, a local restauranteur, led the committee. Well over 100 people were involved in the making of "Ambrosia & Nectar."

To write about "Ambrosia & Nectar," I felt I had to try out as many recipes as possible. I enlisted some help from family.

I made the Eggplant Casserole (moussaka.) My cousins did Wine Dipped Meat Balls (soutzoukakia) and marinated mushrooms. My mother made beef onion stew (stifado) and a Lima Bean salad (using the aptly named Gigantes beans.) My aunts made Green Bean Salad, cheese-filled triangles (tiropitakia), and a dessert made with shredded wheat cereal (mock kataiffi.) I also made Koulourakia, an Easter cookie that uses ammonia for leavening. (A recipe for these appears in my 2023 book "Festive Maryland Recipes: Holiday Traditions from the Old Line State.")

In 2023, Greek Orthodox Easter falls on April 16th, one week after other Christian churches celebrate Easter. Following a special midnight service at the Cathedral of the Annunciation, families will gather to feast and crack red Easter eggs.

There is one section of "Ambrosia & Nectar" that I did not try make any recipes from... yet. Towards the back of the book, there is an illustration of a crab and the title "Favorite Maryland Recipes." The pages that follow contain beaten biscuits, Maryland Fried Chicken, Lady Baltimore Cake, crab soup, crab cakes, crab imperial plus some crab, crab, and more crab!

Though separated in the book, these recipes were made in the same kitchens as grapevine leaves stuffed with rice, silky Avgolemono soup made with egg and lemon, and Easter Soup containing lamb lung. "Ambrosia & Nectar" is yet another testament to the infinite range of Maryland kitchens. And to the irresistibility of Maryland crab. ✳

Eggplant Casserole (Moussaka)

2 large eggplants	**Cream Sauce:**
1 1/2 pounds ground beef	6 tablespoons flour
2 medium onions, chopped	1 quart milk
2 cloves garlic, chopped	1 teaspoon salt
1 can tomato paste	1/8 pound butter
1 can water	1/4 cup grated cheese
salt & pepper	6 eggs
1 teaspoon sugar	

Slice and soak the eggplants in cold salted water for 1 hour. Drain, wipe dry and fry in vegetable oil until light brown. Drain on paper towels.

Brown ground beef for ten minutes, add onions and garlic and brown for five more minutes. Add tomato sauce, water, salt and pepper, and sugar and let cook until liquid evaporates.

Brown flour in saucepan, add butter, milk, salt, and grated cheese. Cook until thickened. Beat eggs until light. Slowly whisk cream sauce into eggs, beating well.

In a casserole dish or pan, place one layer of eggplant, sprinkle with grated cheese, and add a layer of meat mixture, then another layer of eggplant. Continue alternating layers. Pour cream sauce over casserole. Bake in 375° oven until browned on top. Allow to cool before serving.

Recipe adapted from "Ambrosia & Nectar," 1962, by Annunciation Greek Orthodox Community,

A COLLECTION OF FAVORITE GREEK RECIPES

Boiled Rock with Egg Sauce, Evelyn Harris

Posted on November 28, 2021

"Next to loving, I suppose that eating is the most fascinating as well as the most deadly form of indoor sport practiced in America, or anywhere. Perhaps I should have placed eating first, for many folks have dyspepsia so badly that they have forgotten how to love and are so disagreeable that no one loves them either." - The Barter Lady: A Woman Farmer Sees It Through

According to Evelyn Harris herself, she had a reputation among the seasonal farm workers of Kent County: "Miss Eveline sure feeds you well." Harris had learned some of her recipes from her mother-in-law, Margaret Harris (née Grier) who, like her, was originally from Baltimore but moved to the Eastern Shore to become a "farmer's wife."

Evelyn was born Mary Evelyn Bockmiller in 1884 to Charles Howard and Jessie H. Bockmiller. Her family lived at 1500 E Lafayette in Baltimore City. At age 10, Evelyn later said, she had "helped to build the Methodist Church at North avenue and Caroline street by selling homemade candy." In later years, she would describe childhood summers spent selling snowballs with syrups made from flavorings and cornstarch. Her product, she recalled in 1918, had been "about as good as ice cream."

She graduated from Eastern Female High School in 1903. The Baltimore Sun regularly mentioned her name in relation to musical performances. Her 1906 wedding engagement announcement said she had been a music teacher for "a number of years." Evelyn had been attending the Peabody Conservatory, but halted her musical education to marry a Kent County farmer named Arthur Livingston Harris. After moving to the Eastern Shore, Evelyn played organ at Betterton Methodist Church, which shared pastors with nearby Still Pond Methodist Church. Still Pond Methodist produced the cookbook that this recipe came from, and that church cemetery is where Evelyn and her husband are buried. Arthur came from a prominent farming family. His own father, whose parents had moved to Maryland from Delaware in 1838, was "one of the pillars of the Methodist Church in the village of Still Pond," according to a 1914 obituary in the Kent News of Chestertown.

Evelyn was an outspoken woman who used her position as a farmer's wife to engage local papers with many letters and, eventually, impassioned columns. In 1914 she wrote an article in the Country Gentleman magazine touting the benefits of a Home Economics course she'd taken at a state college. There, she's learned about new devices like a vacuum cleaner. She'd learned about bacteria in the kitchen, and thermometer readings for safety. She'd also learned about how store-bought preserves contained artificial ingredients, and about the science of bread-rising. Her friends, she said, were astonished that she would enroll in a home economics course. "You [know] how to cook as well as anyone around here!," they told her, and she happily conceded that she did in fact know how to cook well, but that "perhaps [she] could learn how to do it more easily."

A 1918 article in the Country Gentleman went into great detail about the canning business that Evelyn operated out of Howell's Point, the farm she ran with her husband. In that article, Evelyn gave her interviewer, Maude Radford Warren, more information than she probably asked for, and emphasized that her husband was "her business partner." A 1915 ad in the Sun mentioned jams, jellies, and eggs for sale, delivered from Howell's Point. Later ads mention Christmas trees, and fruit – especially pears. Around 1928, Howells Point was one of the largest pear tree orchards in the eastern United States.

Evelyn's many letters and columns attempted to educate readers on the plight of farmers. She complained of being asked to reduce production while producers of "synthetic butter, imitation preserves, imported powdered milk, or imported powdered eggs" were not. She described the lack of access to resources and education, compared to when she'd lived in the big city. In one famous controversial column, she advocated for "plural wives" for farmers, 'one for every 40 acres', to spread the burden of hard work. The idea was probably meant to draw attention to the hard-working life of farm women... and almost certainly to stir the pot.

In 1923, Governor Ritchie appointed Evelyn Harris to his agricultural committee, so that her concerns could have more direct impact on policy. But not everyone was a fan of Evelyn's ideas, or at least of her writing voice. In 1923, a Baltimore Sun reader wrote in response to one of Evelyn Harris' columns:

"No doubt that many readers who have never had the pleasure of becoming acquainted with Mrs. Harris think she is most wonderful and eagerly await her articles as they are published from time to time, but to we poor folk down here on the Sho' that do happen to know her — well, it's a joke. We think it about time for some one to put a silencer on her stuff." The letter was signed simply and ominously, "One Who Knows."

The 2015 book "Legendary Locals of Kent County," by Patricia Joan O. Horsey described Mrs. Harris as "controversial and colorful."

In 1924, Arthur Harris died. Evelyn's voice changed from that of the "farmer's wife," to a widow running and managing the farm herself, scraping to get by. Evelyn supported her family by making trades – corn cobs for haircuts and chickens for a book club subscription. She became known as "The Barter Lady."

Her collected columns from this era eventually were published in 1934 as a book, "The Barter Lady: A Woman Farmer Sees It Through."

In May 1929 the Sun ran a full-page spread interview with Evelyn. This was before the Bay Bridge was built, and Evelyn had "now adopted the airplane as a means of advancing her farming interests." The idea was ahead of its time, and the article exclaimed: "Just to think of having a ripe luscious Bartlett or Madame D'Anjou plopped down upon your breakfast tables right out of an orchard across the bay!" Evelyn's son piloted the plane, which enabled them to fly directly to Baltimore to call out buyers who tried to cheat them by claiming the pears had gone bad. By 1930, Evelyn's columns mentioned her desire to get her own pilot's license.

The columns are full of local details, such as her family's Chesapeake Bay water dog, "given to [her] as a puppy in trade for a bite which [the dog's] mother took from [Evelyn's] leg." She reminisced about bringing the "first portable moving-picture machine" to Kent County "before the talkies had started." She complained of the scourge of wealthy men from the city buying up farms and operating them as vanity projects.

On food she mentioned wild goose and duck, and that "most of us like to eat the little fat 'muskrats' as they are called in this locality, and when properly handled they are really good to eat."

She favored homemade foods for political reasons and as a matter of taste. "Bakers' bread has caused more divorces than have hot biscuits or hot waffles or hot rolls," she wrote, anecdotally describing an incident in which a burglar was scared away by a can of biscuits randomly exploding.

In a typical attention-getting column, Evelyn bragged that her chicken house was made from the scaffold used to hang four of the suspects in the "famous Hill Murder," an 1892 incident in which nine Black men and boys were accused of murdering a white doctor.

Taking wood from what amounted to a lynching wasn't the only way that Evelyn Harris benefited off of the suffering of Black people. Harris may have been outspoken but she was not enlightened. Her book espouses condescending, racist views on her Black neighbors, claiming they had "no idea how to stretch a dollar," while admitting that she sometimes traded them food for chores instead of paying them money.

Although Evelyn's writing career seemed to exemplify "rural versus urban" tensions that fomented in the early 20th century, she eventually returned to Baltimore. In 1944 she was living at 4437 Clifton Road, had just taken up study at the Peabody again, and was profiled in the Sun decrying most singers' abilities to sing the national anthem. "High G is Low Barrier," the headline read.

Yet another newspaper profile in 1952 called Mrs. Harris an "advocate of musical therapy," and said that she was back at Betterton for the summer, selling sticky buns, gingerbread, coffee cake, and potato rolls.

That would be her last major newspaper profile, although, in the years leading up to her 1967 death, she continued to write to the

Sun to advocate for musical therapy, complain about postal rates, and to decry the fact that a prospective hotel claimed the need of a liquor license to turn a profit. The license applicants, the Charles House Company, she wrote, had "never eaten any real honest-to-goodness Maryland crab cakes, fried chicken or hot potato rolls." The owners of the would-be hotel "can't imagine chicken salad with homemade salad dressing." "Of course," she lamented "most of their customers-to-be will not have had this pleasure either."

I've only scratched the surface of Evelyn's many, many strong opinions and adventures. "The Barter Lady" offers a lot of interesting insight into Eastern Shore culture at the start of the Great Depression, and a timeless slice human nature. ❀

Boiled Rock With Egg Sauce

Wrap rock in large cloth, drop in boiling salted water for about 30 minutes. Take immediately out of water, place on dish and surround with sauce made as follows: Boil hard six eggs, remove and mash fine the yolks. Add two tablespoons of butter, one-half teaspoonful of salt, one-quarter teaspoonful pepper, one-half teaspoonful mustard. Have a pint of hot milk, cut whites of eggs fine and when milk begins to boil, add the other mixture, and the whites, stirring all the time to prevent lumping. When thick pour over the fish.

Recipe from "The Eastern Shore Cook Book, of Maryland Recipes"

Evelyn Harris author photo from her 1924 book

Rose Geranium Cake, Mary B. Shellman

Posted on April 10, 2022

Note: This is the cake shown on my appearance on CBS Mornings, September 16, 2021

Robert H. Clark was one of the two-thirds of Civil War fatalities who died not from the violence on the battlefield, but of disease. The Canada-born Union soldier enlisted in the 7th Maine Infantry in August 1862 at the age of 23. He left behind his wife Mary Ann and one-year-old baby Henry Gilbert, and headed for Maryland. The Maine 7th took part in the Maryland Campaign and a battle at South Mountain, before fighting at Antietam, a significant and bloody turning point in the war.

Constant campaigning had cost the regiment the loss of many men. They returned to Portland, Maine through January of 1863 before reporting to Northern Virginia for more fighting, including the Union victory at the Second Battle of Fredericksburg. In June, the company would pass through Maryland on their way to the fateful battle at Gettysburg. As it happened, Robert H. Clark would never make it to Pennsylvania.

Sources differ on whether the young man had contracted typhoid or died from sunstroke. According to Lt. Colonel Selden Connor, men "fell out by scores... by the heat, dust and exertion" on the trip, some dying in the road.

Clark made it to a hotel in Westminster Maryland, where he was tended to by Mary Bostwick Shellman, a 14-year old who routinely volunteered with the care, feeding and entertainment of residents of the town almshouse. That day, the dutiful girl was caring for soldiers at the City Hotel, which was inundated with infirm men passing through town between battles. She fanned Clark for hours, but it was in vain. Young Mary Shellman watched as Robert Clark died. She would never forget the experience.

Born in 1849, Mary B. Shellman was one of four children born to Westminster citizens Catherine Jones and Col. James M. Shellman. At 14, Shellman was already shaping up to be the stuff of local legend. It's said that one of the first entities she crusaded to memorialize was a sycamore tree, sentenced to be cut to make way for a road. Shellman persuaded the mayor to rename the lane Sycamore Street in the tree's honor.

Shortly before her experience tending to the Union soldier Robert Clark, J.E.B. Stuart greeted Shellman and a group of Westminster children and was apparently rebuffed. Stories vary, but in one, she replied "I'm southern by birth but Yankee in principle," irritating the Confederate general. In another she mocked him by calling him "Johnny Red Coat."

At one point, passing herself off as "M.B. Shellman", Mary started Westminster's first boy scout troop, serving as a scoutmaster until the organization found out her gender.

As telephone lines made their way into towns like Westminster, Mary made sure her home was the first residence in Carroll county to have one. She became the manager of the regional division of the Chesapeake and Potomac Telephone Company. When Alexander Graham Bell came to inspect the system, he gave Mary a telephone pin, which remained among her possessions and became a part of her legend.

Shellman had another pin in her collection —a Red Cross Pin, care of Clara Barton— earned in 1889 when Mary joined Marylanders who rushed to Pennsylvania to assist in the aftermath of the Johnstown Flood.

Mary was a suffragette, also championing suffrage's companion cause, temperance. Stereotypes aside, she seemed to have some fun. After Christmas of 1865, she wrote to a cousin in Frederick, describing a joyful holiday party spent dancing with "would you believe it... a returned Reb." She playfully mentioned a visit from "a fair-haired friend," and her eagerness to meet his friends.

"Rose Geranium Cake" is one of four recipes that Shellman contributed to "Choice Maryland Cookery," a 1902 cookbook compiled by the women of St. Paul Lutheran Church in Uniontown. Her other recipes are for a horehound "Cough Remedy"", Pink Watermelon Preserves, and Pineapple Marmalade. Shellman's interest in food continued during the first World War, when she worked in Herbert Hoover's Food

Administration.

In the 1920s, Shellman did work preserving Westminster's history, laying the groundwork for the institutions that preserve her own memory to this day. The "Sherman-Fisher-Shellman House" where she grew up is now a property of the Carroll County Historical Society. She wrote a book on Westminster history that is in the collections of the Pratt Library and the Maryland Center for History and Culture. The latter library houses an additional history manuscript she wrote, as well as some poems and letters. A plaque honoring her suffrage work was unveiled in Westminster in December 2021.

Mary's motley life was also peppered with the arts. She performed in community theater and wrote poetry, including lyrics to a rally song for William McKinley's 1900 presidential campaign, a poem honoring the life of Nicholas Paroway (a Westminster citizen who was born into slavery in Baltimore), and a memorial hymn for Arlington National Cemetery.

The hymn reflects Mary's lasting effort to honor the lives and deaths of soldiers.

In May 1868, when Mary was 18, she responded to a call from Union veterans' organization commander Gen. John A. Logan to decorate the graves of soldiers. She led an assembly of local children through town on their way to Westminster Cemetery to lay flowers on soldier's graves. "Decoration Day" eventually became Memorial Day, and Mary Shellman would remain involved in Westminster's Memorial Day Parade for the next 60 years. Five Union soldiers are buried in a plot that Shellman set aside to spare the men from "pauper burials." Robert H. Clark's grave marker is the first and the largest.

The death that cemented Mary B. Shellman's commitment to honor fallen soldiers remained personal. In the 1880s, Shellman corresponded with Henry Gilbert Clark, Robert's son. One of the countless children left fatherless by the Civil War, Henry Clark had been just an infant when Robert left for war. Henry's mother lost custody or abandoned him after the war, and he was raised by family. Historians' attempts to trace his later life and whereabouts dead-end at 1924.

Mary isn't buried near the soldiers at Westminster. In later life, she moved to live near her nephew Rev. Paul Reese in Rockland Texas. She died in 1938, shortly after instituting Memorial Day ceremonies there. She is buried in Rockland Cemetery.

I didn't do much of my own primary-source research for this. There is just too much. Volunteers at the Historical Society of Carroll County have worked to chronicle the varied events in the life of Mary B. Shellman and of those she came into contact with. It's a wide web with threads cast via the memorialization of the casualties of the Civil War, of the history of the telephone, the Red Cross, of votes for women, a street named Sycamore, and now, by a cake recipe. ❋

Rose Geranium Cake

One cup butter, one pound A sugar, yolks of six eggs, whites of four eggs, one cup cold water, three and one-half cups sifted flour, three teaspoons Royal baking powder. Cream butter and sugar together, add yolks and beat well, then stir in the water. Beat whites of eggs to a stiff froth; sift baking powder in flour; add whites of eggs and flour, alternately; stir well, but do not beat. Grease and flour two mountain cake pans, lay three rose geranium leaves in each, pour the batter on them and bake in moderate oven. Use the whites of the two eggs left from the cake for iceing, and flavor iceing with vanilla. When the cake is baked, remove geranium leaves before putting cakes together. Put iceing between layers, on top and sides. The leaves give a delicious flavor.
MISS MARY B. SHELLMAN

Recipe from "Choice Maryland Cookery", Printed at the Caroll Record Office, 1902

Potato Salad, Thomasina Falcon

Posted on June 7, 2018

"Western High May Become Coeducational Negro School," the 1954 Baltimore Sun Headline read. Hand-wringing about school desegregation was splashed throughout the pages of the Sun that year. The issue that brought Western High to the front line of the fight was its status as an all-girls school. If the quality of education was unique in white single-sex institutions, then "separate but equal" was subject to question. The NAACP was challenging Baltimore Polytechnic Institute's unique engineering program on similar grounds.

Enrollment had been dropping at Western, as its surrounding West Baltimore neighborhood became populated with Black families whose daughters were barred from the school. Elizabeth T. Meijer of the Baltimore Urban League suggested the obvious solution – integrate the school. She wrote to the Sun that Baltimore was in a position to "not only show the U.S.A. but the whole world... that we not only preach but practice democracy." Making Western High School an integrated girls' school was not apparently seriously considered by the school board. There was talk of closing the school altogether.

Ultimately it was decided that the school would relocate to the old City College location at Howard and Centre Streets. Frederick Douglass High School moved into Western's old location on Gwynns Falls Road.

Thankfully, not everyone was satisfied with this outcome. In June 1953, Eugene D. Byrd wrote a passionate letter to the Sun chastising the school board for hiding behind "ancient views... of persons who cannot understand that God is Love and all mankind is the same in His sight."

A few years later, a 1956 Sun report declared that the public had accepted the integration of schools, despite a flurry of agitators picketing and student absenteeism in September. By the 1960s, Western High School yearbooks exhibited an integrated student population, united by a common penchant for bouffant hair shellacked meticulously skyward.

Western High School remains a girls' school to this day; the oldest public all-girls school in the United States (Eastern having gone coed in the early 80s.)

In 1971, Mrs. Sarah Cooper's senior English class found out that the teacher was unfamiliar with soul food. The girls began to bring in dishes for Mrs. Cooper to enjoy. Eventually, the students even commandeered the home economics room, inviting the principal and vice principal to dine. "You couldn't miss what was going on in that room," said Cooper, "The whole school smelled of soul food."

With the help of guidance counselor Maisie Rea, the social exchange became a project – the "Soul Food Cookbook." Rea later explained to Baltimore Sun reporter Jane Howard: "There is no mild tasting soul food. It is more in the way food is seasoned that distinguishes it... we can fix the same dish but mine wouldn't taste like yours." Rea's recipe for kidney stew is included in the book. "People of today rarely have time for the long, slow processes that were responsible for the tasty stews... of earlier days," she wrote. "Members of my family, however, have held on to some of our traditional recipes."

The book contains recipes for cracklin' cornbread, hog maws and chit'lins, black-eyed peas, and coconut pie, along with less famous dishes like peach upside-down cake and "caramel eggnog."

This potato salad recipe was contributed to the book by Thomasina Falcon. Unfortunately, I couldn't find much about her although I believe she was originally from Anson County North Carolina. She passed away in 1986.

In addition to the recipes, the "Soul Food Cookbook" is peppered with poetry and personal stories about family and food. Mrs. Beulah Taylor wrote that her recipe for cabbage with fatback drippings had been "handed down from generation to generation... as many times as [the] recipe has been handed down, it still tastes good every time." ❊

Potato Salad

12 medium white potatoes, diced
2 diced onions
1.5 stalks diced celery
2 carrots, shredded
6 diced pickles
1.5 Tablespoons mustard
2.5 Teaspoons celery seed

4 Tablespoons mayonnaise
2 Tablespoons salt
1 Teaspoon pepper
2 Teaspoons sugar
1 Teaspoons vinegar
2 Teaspoons pickle juice
1 green pepper

Bring potatoes to boil about 20 minutes until soft, but not too soft. Place potatoes in drainer and then put in refrigerator, after all the water is drained out. While potatoes are cooking, cut up onions, celery, carrots, pickles, and green pepper. Let potatoes stay in the refrigerator for about 1 hour or until cold. Put onions, celery, pickles, carrots and green pepper in the refrigerator. Take out potatoes, cut them into cubes, and put them in large mixing bowl. Then add your onions, celery, and pickles, carrots and green pepper to potatoes and mix lightly. Next add celery seed, sugar, salt, pepper, and pickle juice and mix together. Then add mayonnaise (or Miracle Whip) and mustard and mix and stir together lightly. Add your vinegar a little at a time and mix. After salad is ready, put it back in the refrigerator so that potatoes can absorb seasonings until you are ready to serve. Garnish potato salad with lettuce, tomatoes, and radishes."

Recipe from The Soul Food Cook Book, 1971, Western High School, found at the Enoch Pratt Free Library

First Row L-R, Sitting: M. Ward, P. Porter, A. Jones, B. Odonis, M. Williams, C. Shockley, D. Fields, D. Bryson, Second Row L-R, Kneeling: Rawls, D. Loats, T. Falcon, M. Johnson, B. Tillery, D. White, B. Donelly, V. Chenowith, Back Row, L-R.: D. Swanson, A. Conaway, A. Bevens, Carter, D. Fortkiewicz, D. Dirion.

Kneeling in the center with the black shirt and white vest is a "T. Falcon," 1970 Western High yearbook

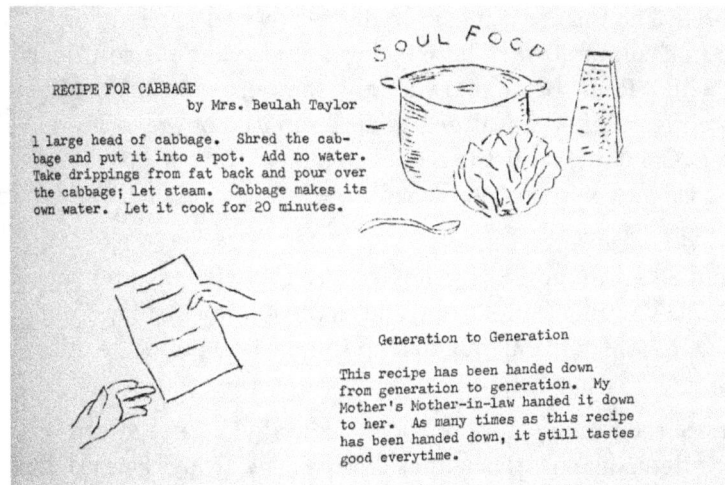

RECIPE FOR CABBAGE
by Mrs. Beulah Taylor

1 large head of cabbage. Shred the cabbage and put it into a pot. Add no water.
Take drippings from fat back and pour over
the cabbage; let steam. Cabbage makes its
own water. Let it cook for 20 minutes.

SOUL FOOD

Generation to Generation

This recipe has been handed down
from generation to generation. My
Mother's Mother-in-law handed it down
to her. As many times as this recipe
has been handed down, it still tastes
good everytime.

Strawberry Shortcake Lida A. Willis (Baltimore Cooking School)

Posted on June 16, 2017

"If alum is something to be proud of why conceal it on the label in type as small as the law permits?" – Alum in Baking Powder, 1927, Royal Baking Powder Company

"Today, the Royal Company is manufacturing and selling a phosphate type of powder such as they condemned and classed as a mineral poison a few years ago." – The Truth About Baking Powder, 1928, Calumet Baking Powder Company

The libraries of Johns Hopkins don't always have much to offer when it comes to my research. This recipe was a rare exception. I found a lot of reports and books about baking powder in the Hopkins Sheridan Libraries. I soon learned that this is because it exists in the grey area between food, chemical, and – some once believed – toxin. It was a potential cause for medical concern.

I selected two books: "Alum in Baking Powder," published by the Royal Baking Powder Company in 1927, and "The Truth About Baking Powder," from the Calumet Baking Powder Company in 1928. The former is meant to dispel any bad publicity or residual rumors from a 1926 Federal Trade Commission Hearing regarding Royal Baking Powder and their crusade against the ingredient alum. The latter book is a rebuttal of the former, in which Calumet wants the reader to look at the cutthroat tactics of Royal and wonder "just what are you so afraid of, Royal Baking Powder?"

If that all seems confusing, its because it is. "Baking Powder Wars," by Linda Civitello chronicles the bumpy history of baking powder from convenient godsend to (alleged) public health menace to kitchen staple.

A lot of recipes in older cookbooks contain long-forgotten ingredients like pearlash and saleratus. I've always been struck by the ingenuity of cooks of that era, and the way that information and ingredients would disseminate around the country. In the case of these baking powder predecessors, they had some help from cookbook authors like Eliza Leslie and Amelia Simmons. Use of these leaveners marked further diversion from American cooking's British roots.

"American women should be given more credit for what they created and for the chemical experiments they conducted in their kitchens. Even if pearlash was not revolutionary by itself – which it was – the accretion of innovation created a new American cuisine." – Baking Powder Wars, Linda Civitello

Aside from chemical leaveners and yeast, you may recall that another traditional way to get air into breads, especially in Maryland, is to beat the hell out of the dough for a half hour or more. Performing this process definitely makes one think of the history of servitude and slavery in Maryland, and Civitello draws a connection between that and Eliza Leslie's distaste for Maryland Biscuits, which Leslie deemed unwholesome (despite including the recipe in her book). Leslie's Maryland contemporary, Elizabeth Ellicott Lea, also an abolitionist Quaker, simply declared that Maryland Biscuits are "very nice for tea." But hey, as Leslie said "there's not accounting for tastes."

Commercial baking powders were first developed in the mid-1800s, even before a reliable yeast was available to consumers. Housewives, cooks and bakers cultivated and maintained their own yeast. Between the different blends of flour, the variability of yeasts, and the makeshift baking powders, we can scarcely imagine the inconsistency of 19th century baked goods.

Regardless, according to Civitello, many women were skeptical of the chemicals, or else fiercely set in their independent ways. The burgeoning baking powder industry resorted to creative means to market their products to consumers.

The Royal Baking Powder Company released a cookbook in 1877, pushing their products with the allure of exciting new recipes. The book disparaged other baking powder formulas and offered hundreds of recipes featuring their product.

As competition heated up, the war began. Royal promoted evidence that the ingredients in other baking powder formulations were responsible for indigestion. The most famous of this 'evidence' involved an 1880 study in which dogs were fed biscuits made with the different baking powder formulas – the Royal formula versus the "other leading brands" containing alum.

"Eight [alum baking powder] biscuits were given to dogs Nos. II and VI in the morning; in the afternoon dog No. II was very loose in his bowels, and dog No. VI very constipated. Five more biscuits were given in the afternoon and eight more the following morning, part of which were eaten. Both the dogs then were extremely constipated and apparently quite sick, although they did not vomit. To-day dog No. IV, in perfect health, was then given three biscuits… the dog became quite sick and vomited. In the afternoon and the next morning more biscuits were given him, but he would not eat." – The Sanitarian, Volume 8, 1880

Very scientific. Loose stools AND constipation?!?! Even a DOG wouldn't eat those biscuits!! Well I say! I'm smarter than a dog!

Nonetheless, the baking powder competition waged on; right on up to the Federal Trade Commission hearing in 1926.

Rumford Chemical Works, whose creator Eben Horsford pioneered the original commercial baking powder formula, produced their own cookbook in 1895. Newspapers around the country advertised a "New Pastry Cook Book" by Baltimore Cooking School principal "L. A. Willis" which could be obtained, for free, from Rumford Chemical Works if you sent in a label (aka your 'proof of purchase') from Horsford Bread Preparation (an early self-rising enriched flour).

Rumford was wisely capitalizing on the rising popularity of cooking instructors, and the cooking instructors capitalized right back.

Lida Ames Willis had been a pupil of Sarah Tyson Rorer, and made good on her credentials with a healthy amount of endorsements. She assisted with Gas & Electric company promotions, and also endorsed Knox Gelatine and Cottolene shortening. Alongside Rorer, Marion Harland, and a few other cooking instructors, Willis contributed recipes to a 1914 book called "Home Helps" – a promotion for Cottolene.

Similar refrains from Cottolene about purity and indigestion make one wonder if there aren't larger forces at play than some unsafe ingredient in baking powder.

Why did people used to suffer from so much indigestion? Well, for starters, nearly any ingredient in a recipe could have been adulterated or spoiled. Refrigeration was not widespread, canning practices were not standardized, and unscrupulous corporate activity was rampant. Maybe people had un-diagnosed sensitivities to gluten or FODMAPs. Maybe e. coli was all over everything (ew). But also... maybe humans just get a lot of indigestion?

Safety concerns are one of the pillars of marketing to this day – GMOs being just one obvious example. And my Rumford Baking Powder tin assures me that the product is aluminum free.

The convenience of baking powder didn't eliminate the use of yeast, or even the tradition of beaten biscuits. Still, we have baking powder to thank for a world of cakes with a light texture and what culinary historian Karen Hess calls a "faint metallic trace of bitterness" that "unfortunately, Americans grew to love."

If you're wondering what happened to the dogs who ate biscuits made with Royal Baking Powder, well: "each dog was given as many biscuits as he would eat... Their bowels were not in the least affected." Those dogs ate a ton of delicious biscuits "with appetite," and their stools were perfect, which is more than I can say about my own dog who eats food that is made for dogs. ✿

Strawberry Shortcake

2 heaping teaspoons baking powder
1 Teaspoon salt
1 Quart flour
2 oz butter plus more for spreading on cake
cold milk
sugared strawberries
whipped cream
Sift 2 heaping teaspoonfuls Rumford Yeast Powder, and 1 teaspoonful salt with 1 quart flour. Rub in 2 ounces butter and moisten to a very soft dough with cold milk. Mix quickly and lightly; pat out into a large round cake 2 inches thick; place in a large, square baking-pan and bake in a very quick oven 20 minutes. While hot pull apart; spread both halves with good, sweet butter, not pressing but dropping it on with a knife; spread the lower half with a thick layer of slightly crushed, sugared strawberries; put on the top crust, dust with sugar, heap with sweetened, whipped cream and garnish with a few large berries. Serve at once, and cut with a hot knife.

Recipe from The Rumford Bread and Pastry Cook by Lida A. Willis

---

Maryland Fried Chicken

Posted on August 13, 2018

"Through the years, Maryland whiskey has become almost as renowned as Maryland fried chicken." – Maryland: A Guide to the Old Line State, Writers' Program of the Works Progress Administration, 1940

In July 1945, war correspondent Ollie Stewart wrote to the Afro-American about the frenzied scene in Berlin as American soldiers had raided Hitler's "medal room" for souvenirs while the Russians looked on, laughing. "We must have looked silly as hell," the journalist remarked.

Stewart left Berlin for Paris, where he'd just missed a banquet for the leaders of the Red Cross. The seven-course feast was served by an all-black staff – a new and novel experience for the Frenchmen. Although Stewart was at a loss to recall the full menu, owing to "so much French in the darn thing," one dish stood out as "the big noise": "Poulet frit Maryland."

According to Stewart, the dish set a new standard for Parisian chefs. Some of them asked him "where is this place, Maryland?" The Afro-American shared the anecdote under the headline: "Maryland Gains Fame."

Of all of the forgotten Maryland recipes, Maryland Fried Chicken may be the most misunderstood. It may even be impossible to understand. Since its nebulous inception, there has been little agreement on just what constitutes "Maryland Fried Chicken," also known as "Fried Chicken, Maryland Style," or sometimes "Chicken a la Maryland." See? There isn't even agreement on what to call it.

When, in 1926, a writer for the Evening Sun playfully proposed a monument to the originator of Maryland Fried Chicken, a column was dedicated to discussing its origin. "The one thing that most endears the Maryland Free State to an admiring world is the succulent flesh of a young hen fried a la Maryland," wrote the anonymous columnist. The state owed an obligation to the dish's progenitor.

Allegedly (and presumably facetiously), the Baltimore Chief Police Detective was called to investigate the inventor of Maryland Fried Chicken, and came up fruitless. Nancy W. Pennington of the Maryland Historical Society was similarly at a loss. She instead offered up her favorite recipe. Home Economist Helen G. Andres refused the question altogether. "I come from Pennsylvania," was her reply. Stewards from the Belvedere & the Rennert shrugged at the question. Charles F. Broehm of the Rennert balked at the monument idea, remarking "if you did put up a memorial, you'd probably put it up to some old Negro mammy. That's probably where Maryland fried chicken got its start."

With this racist statement, Broehm arrived the closest thing to the truth. Despite his paradoxically dismissive attitude towards the culinary traditions to which he owed his very livelihood, the hotel steward remained cognizant of their origin. While Broehm declared that chicken "a la Maryland" was not "the artistic creation that pate de foie gras is," others took delight in the worldwide fame of a dish bearing the name of our state. As Ollie Stewart's recollection suggests, Maryland Fried Chicken was a central player in the decades-long cultural cold war between French chefs and Black American caterers.

In "Soul Food: The Surprising Story of An American Cuisine," Adrian Miller explored the evolution of fried chicken from West African and British cooking traditions. "Two states laid claim to having the best method" to fry chickens, wrote Miller. The Virginia method involved pork in the fat for flavor, whereas the Maryland method entails covering the chicken while it fries, adding steam for moisture. The final product is then served with gravy and waffles or fritters.

The steaming step does feature in many Maryland recipes, but it is far from synonymous with Maryland Fried Chicken. Fritters, waffles, or fried mush are frequently but not always specified. Some recipes contain batter or egg. In others, the chicken is merely seasoned and floured. Even the cream gravy is in dispute.

In his 1951 history of Baltimore, "The Amiable Baltimoreans," F. F. Beirne admitted that "in spite of all the enthusiastic praise of chicken á la Maryland, the scandal is that few persons even in Baltimore actually know what it is."

Beirne referred to the cream gravy and fried mush but admitted that some "fully authenticated Baltimoreans with generations of Maryland lineage behind them will tell you cream gravy is no part of true chicken a la Maryland."

Mrs. Leigh Zerbee shared a fried chicken recipe in the Baltimore Sun in 1946. The chicken was fried, steamed in the pan, and served with cream gravy. The chicken was actually cooked by Cora Holland.

Novelist and domestic expert Marion Harland wrote a column in the Oakland Tribune in 1909 which asserted that "Maryland Fried Chicken" was a "palpable misnomer." She implied that a more accurate name would be "Virginia Fried Chicken with Cream Gravy." Harland was from Virginia.

Searching digitized newspapers provides anecdotal evidence at best, but it does suggest that Maryland was first associated with fried chicken around 1880, a few years before our neighbor to the south. An 1885 recipe for "Fried Chicken Maryland Style," printed in the Midland Journal in Rising Sun Maryland, features a dusting of flour, cream gravy, no fritters.

A debate over Maryland versus Virginia fried chicken may be a bit too strenuous if no one can agree what the dish in question even IS. In 1911, the New York Sun declared that Maryland Fried Chicken was representing the entire country to the world. "Cook books in half of the civilized countries on the globe pay tribute to it," they wrote, "but no two of the receipts are alike."

This state of confusion may be partly responsible for why you may not have heard of Maryland Fried Chicken today. A vanishing Southern chain has kept the name in the phone book for a few decades, seemingly without any of the features that allegedly make fried chicken "Maryland." Chef and cookbook author John Shields has perhaps done the most to re-popularize Maryland Fried Chicken through his recipes and his restaurant Gertrude's, which serves up Maryland Pan-fried Chicken on Tuesday nights.

The fact that the chicken is only a weekly event is telling.

Another major reason that Maryland Fried Chicken is hard to come by is the relative time and effort it takes to pan fry versus deep frying. When the onus is on restaurants to keep our traditions alive, we end up sacrificing much in the name of convenience and cost-effectiveness.

This is the part where I implore you to join me in defending Maryland Fried Chicken. "But Kara," you say, "you never decided what in the hell Maryland Fried Chicken really is!" Well... do you like cream gravy? Then demand it! Corn fritters? Insist upon them! Do you frequently find yourself with a lot of leftover mush? Fry that mush, and fry some chicken. Nothing establishes authenticity like contention and stubbornness.

There is only one hard and fast rule: whatever you want Maryland Fried Chicken to be, be passionate about it. Be vocal and steadfast in your unwavering opinion. And accept no substitutes. ✿

Fried Chicken, Maryland Style

"Have the chickens killed the day before they are to be eaten and put on ice. Cut the chicken in seven pieces, have them wiped dry, then flour lightly, season high with pepper and salt. Have your lard boiling hot, then put the chicken in, turning carefully, let it soak well, then take it out, and put in a pan to keep hot. Then have some flour browned, and add to the gravy in the pan with a good cup full of cream or rich milk with some parsley chopped, let it thicken, and serve it in a gravy dish. Make mush cakes, fry separately, serve on the dish with the chicken."

Recipe from Mrs. Charles H. Gibson's Maryland and Virginia Cook Book

"Coralline" Muffins The Practical Cook Book

Posted on February 10, 2020

The Slow Foods Ark of Taste is a list of thousands of food products, collected with the intent of promoting and preserving them before they die out. The list includes heirloom fruits and vegetables, rare livestock breeds, and prepared specialty foods like cheeses. Items are nominated to the list using criteria factoring in uniqueness, sustainability, and quality. The Slow Food USA website declares that "these foods are prized by those who eat them for their special taste." No commercial or trademarked products are selected.

But what about foods that just... aren't that special? What about all of the commercial products that have come and gone, perhaps dying out justly and unlamented? Obsessed as I am with the detritus of popular culture, I can't help but wonder about extinct ingredients that no one publicly mourned.

New Jersey-based Purity Cross offered a wide variety of unique canned specialties in the 1920s: Welsh Rarebit, Lobster a la Newburg, Plum Pudding...

The Pin Money Pickle Company was started by a Richmond woman in 1868 and became a ubiquitous product served by restaurants and caterers. The pickle company died out in the 1950s and 60s amid a sea of competition.

Mrs. B. C. Howard included a recipe in her 1873 "Fifty Years in a Maryland Kitchen" cookbook for a pudding made from a new product produced by the "American Fruit Preserving Company" of Baltimore, Granulated Sweet Potato. Mrs. Howard promised that the product would be in stores "by the 1st of October." Perhaps it was. It's not in stores any longer.

Similarly, the 1888 "Practical Cook Book" by Mrs. J.H. Giese of Baltimore, includes 20+ recipes for an item called "Coralline."

The product is given its own section in the cookbook, and is introduced as though readers will know what it is:

"Handy Receipt! No Cooking! Place desired amount of Coralline dry in a China or Porcelain vessel add sufficient milk or water to cover, and let stand until the Coralline absorbs the liquid. Use custard, cream, sweetened milk, or any flavored dressing desired. Splendid for pic-nics, quick desserts, and a most delightful dish for summer evening teas."

The variety of uses makes things even more confusing: Stir the product into beaten eggs to make "Coralline Omelets." Mix Coralline into bread dough and waffle batter. Use it to make puddings for dessert. Add it to soups and stewed oysters.

A full-page advertisement later in the book reveals that Coralline was not a common pantry staple. "Give it a trial," the ad proposed, "Ask your grocer for it." The patent date is listed as May 4th, 1886. "An entirely new and reliable article of food, made from Southern White Corn. For purity, healthfulness and convenience, it stands unrivaled."

An 1887 ad in the Baltimore Sun was even more over-the-top, asserting that Coralline was "recommended by leading physicians for adults and children," and that the product was "superior to all other food." Pretty superlative for a product that no one has heard of.

Researching Coralline turns up mostly Baltimore-based ads, plus a factory fire in 1887. There was also a lawsuit. When a former business associate began selling a similar product, named "Barlyne," the Maryland Hominy & Coralline Company successfully sued. The resulting document gives some insight into the nature of the Coralline product – as well as the seemingly accidental way it was invented.

The documents describe Coralline as a "product from Indian corn, consisting of separate grains, in a stringy or coralline form," "elongated curled granules," produced by "cooking the product in a moistened condition to a point at which it still retains the granular form, then passing the same, in its moist condition, through a grinding-mill, and finally drying it substantially as described."

Mrs. J. H. Giese solicited advertisements from many other Baltimore businesses in addition to Coralline. Ads appear throughout "The Practical Cook Book" promoting upholstering, coal, groceries, shirts, plumbers, stables, pianos, and specialty purveyors of items like yeast, lard, and beef tongues. "The Practical Cook Book" was so marketing-forward that it was subtitled "... where to buy almost everything pertaining to house-keeping from well established firms." An index of advertisers appeared in the back of the book.

Based on the Library of Congress information about Mrs. Giese's book, I believe her identity to be Catherine Giese, wife of James Henry Giese. Catherine (who sometimes went by 'Kate') was born in 1830 in Pennsylvania to Margaret and James Huling. Her father was a business associate of J. Henry Giese, who married Catherine in 1852. Mr. Giese was a merchant dealing in cement, plaster, and grains. His business is advertised on the inside back cover of the "Practical Cook Book".

Catherine's grandfather Michael Ross was the founder of Williamsport, PA. Catherine and J. Henry had at least four children. Their eldest son Louis became a merchant who also has an ad in the cookbook. Their daughter Florence, born in 1864, was a music teacher who studied at the Peabody Conservatory. Her opinions on music and her students' performances merited frequent mentions in the Baltimore Sun up through the 1940s.

Other than that I don't have much information. The Giese family lived in various locations around the city – most notably 2118 St. Paul Street, where they lived in 1905 when J. Henry died.

Unsurprisingly, some of the recipes in The Practical Cook Book are taken from other familiar cookbooks. A recipe for "Tongue Toast" is swiped from "Mrs. Charles Gibson's Maryland and Virginia Cook Book." Incidentally, an advertisement for a grocer specializing in tongue appeared in the "Practical Cook Book". Could it be that Mrs. Giese went looking for recipes to match the advertisements? It is very likely.

Rumford Chemical Works has a full-paged ad for their baking powder, then known as "Yeast Powder." Like Coralline, Rumford claimed that their product was recommended by "eminent Physicians," and that it was "nutritious and strength-giving." Even today, Rumford boasts that their baking powder is a "source of calcium in your diet." That's great news if you're in the habit of eating entire cakes in one sitting.

The Maryland Hominy & Coralline Company did not have Rumford's longevity. The company dissolved in 1896. A notice in the Baltimore Sun said that the manufacturing of Coralline was abandoned in 1894, when "it had ceased to be profitable." With the factory fire taken into consideration, the most superior food in the world only existed for about five years!

Based on the product described in the lawsuit, I substituted instant grits. The resulting muffins had a nice texture, and they were actually surprisingly moist. In fact, they were so moist that the extra muffins molded within a few days. Like Coralline, their time was numbered, and they were not worth saving. ✽

Coralline Muffins

One pint sifted Flour, two heaping teaspoonfuls of Yeast Powder, and a little Salt. Thoroughly mix together; then add one pint of Coralline, two Eggs, one tablespoonful of Butter, and enough Sweet Milk to make a thick batter. Bake immediately.

Recipe from The Practical Cook Book, Mrs. J. H. Giese, 1888

Augustine's Croquettes, Miss A. C. Claytor

Posted on July 22, 2023

"We do not believe that in the length and breadth of New York there is just such a place of refined enjoyment, dietetically speaking, as that narrow red brick house, not more than twenty feet front, in Walnut street, above Eleventh. It is not Delmonico's in splendor, for there is no splendor, but it is exquisite in its comfort. Let all who go to the Centennial carefully abstain from the cold, badly-cooked edible of the commemorative dinner-tables, make it a point to visit Mr. Peter Augustin. A Centenniel croquette, a Revolutionary ris de veaux, will repay one for a dull day in Philadelphia."

— The Philadelphia Times, 1875

I am guilty of occasionally forgetting that the railroads that brought passengers from points north into Baltimore to enjoy "real old Maryland cooking" ran both ways.

Culinary reminders of this two-way exchange occasionally appear in recipes with names such as "Delmonico Pudding," or "Philadelphia Pepper Pot." Others are less obvious.

Recipes for "Augustine's Croquettes" appear repeatedly throughout my database: in the c.1895-1905 Goldsborough Family Papers recipe manuscript, in "New Old Southern Cooking", written in 1902 by Laura D. Pickenpaugh, and finally, in the 1937 "Recipes Old and New" from St. Anne's Parish cookbook (this recipe was also repeated in Maryland's Way.)

These three recipes provide a hidden reminder that Philadelphia, like Baltimore, was a city where Black caterers had a stronghold over the culinary industry. W.E.B. DuBois wrote in his study "The Philadelphia Negro" that there existed "as remarkable a trade guild as ever ruled in a medieval city. This was the guild of the caterers, and its masters include names which have been household words in the city for fifty years: Bogle, Augustin, Prosser, Dorsey, Jones, and Minton."

Three generations of the Augustin family reigned in Philadelphia, their overlapping careers spanning nearly a century.

In the early 1900s, the Maryland press liked to pit Black chefs against French chefs in a culinary proxy battle from which Maryland/Southern cuisine generally emerged triumphant. This oversimplification loses some intrigue when you remember that plenty of Black chefs were trained in French techniques. The whole thing seems even more silly in light of the fact that the industry was pioneered by men like Peter aka Pierre Augustin, a Creole man from Haiti, who probably was both Black AND French.

Around 1818, Augustin purchased the Philadelphia catering business of Robert Bogle. Bogle is credited with essentially establishing catering as a Black profession, but Augustin is credited with offering services that would become standards of the trade, such as providing china, tablecloths, tables, and chairs for catered events. "Bogle's place was eventually taken by Peter Augustin, a West Indian immigrant, who started a business in 1818 which is still carried on. It was the Augustin establishment that made Philadelphia catering famous all over the country," wrote DuBois.

The Augustin catering empire encompassed several talented family members including Mary Frances, a confectioner, and her and Peter's son James, who ran the business with his mother after Peter's death in 1841. Their restaurant M.F. Augustin & Son, was known as the "Delmonico's of Philadelphia." Peter Jerome Augustin took over the business when his brother James died in 1877.

In 1879, the Philadelphia Times wrote that Augustin & Son "in addition the nightly supper parties at their rooms on Walnut Street, for which the charge is never less than five dollars a plate," provided catering to clients all over the United States, furnishing terrapin, turkey, salads and other "good things" to clients in New York, Boston, Pittsburgh, and Nashville. The business had patrons in "Paris and other European cities."

Of all of the varied viands provided by the Augustin's, one dish won them fame and publicity above all others: their chicken croquettes.

In 1881, Lorenzo Delmonico divulged the culinary preferences of some of his more famous clientele to a New York newspaper. One man, lawyer Charles Brooke, was originally from Philadelphia. According to Delmonico, Brooke had "a tendency to chicken croquettes born of a taste created at Augustin's that should be restrained."

Then as now, people who couldn't make the trip to experience such a much-talked-about dish wanted a taste.

The recipes that made their way to Maryland differ from one another. Goldsborough's contained "chicken or veal", potato, cream, eggs, pepper, salt, nutmeg, and was rolled in "cracker dust". The recipe in Pickenpaugh's cookbook included chicken, sweetbreads, butter, onion, and nutmeg. The recipe I used, submitted by Miss A. C. Claytor to "Recipes Old and New," contained chicken, flour, butter, onion, nutmeg, and parsley.

My recipe is similar to one uncovered in the late 1980s by William Woys Weaver. In his book "Thirty-five Receipts from the Larder Invaded," he printed a recipe from an 1890s manuscript of a Lizzie Martin, an unidentified Philadelphian. Martin recorded "Croquettes Augustine's" alongside her recipe for Philadelphia Pepper Pot. The Lebanon Pennsylvania Daily News printed the recipe in 1987 under the headline "'Long Lost' Croquettes Discovered."

Ingredients aside, this is just the type of recipe that demonstrates the futility of even having recipes for this kind of thing. I imagined the Augustines and their staff's skill at chopping, sauce-making, and frying up hundreds of croquettes night after night. Anyone can combine chicken with some seasonings. It's the process that takes skill.

After Peter Jerome's 1894 death, his wife Elizabeth B. Augustin ran the business. As with her mother-in-law Mary Frances, Elizabeth's career is a reminder that there were many women involved in catering operations, even if they did not get the glory. It is unknown when exactly the Augustin's business ceased operations – probably between 1904 and 1907.

The gilded-age heyday of Black catering may have faded, but its impact has been woven into the hospitality industry we know today. With their aspirations to capture a taste of that prestige in their own kitchens, home cooks left recipes in cookbooks and manuscripts, faint echoes of a time when the "remarkable guild" captured appetites and imaginations. ❁

Augustine's Croquettes

1 chicken, boiled and minced very fine; 1 pint milk, 1 large tablespoon flour, 1/4 pound butter, 1 teaspoon minced onion, a very little nutmeg or some minced parsley, salt and pepper to taste. Make cream sauce of milk, flour, butter and seasoning, and cook until thick; add the chicken and set aside to cool. Shape in molds, roll in bread crumbs, then in beaten egg, then again in bread crumbs, and fry in butter or lard.

Augustine was a famous caterer in his time.

From "Recipes Old and New," St. Anne's Parish, 1937

NINETIETH ANNIVERSARY OF AME-
RICAN INDEPENDENCE.
THE STATE SOCIETY OF THE CINCINNATI, OF PENNSYLVANIA.
The annual stated meeting of the "State Society of the Cincinnati, of Pennsylvania" will be held at Augustin's. No. 1105 WALNUT Street, at 10 o'clock A. M. on Wednesday, July 4, 1866. Members of other State Societies who may be in the city on that day are invited to dine with the Society, at 5 o'clock P. M., at the above place.   GEO. W. HARRIS, Secretary.

1866

Zucchini Spice Cake ala B.G.E.

Posted on January 13, 2023

"We have made several notices of various improvements and inventions for cooking and heating by gas," read an article in the Baltimore Sun in 1854, "and we have no doubt the result will eventually prove important to the world." At a fair in Philadelphia, a gas stove made by Andrew Mayer had been used to roast a 14lb piece of beef for two hours. "The meat was partaken by a number of persons," the Sun wrote, "and highly enjoyed."

Cooking was an ordeal that required the acquisition of wood or coal to heat a stove. Controlling the heat was a challenge. And the inconveniences affected more than just the cook. The fuel produced ash and smoke. Airborne cinders could cause mass destruction.

But gas stoves didn't catch on immediately. In many homes, a stove served other functions, like heating the house. Some gas ranges accounted for this, while others did not. For some people, a cozy open hearth or a radiating wood stove were comforting presences. And learning to cook on a new device doesn't exactly excite people who were tasked with cooking for a family day-in and day-out.

Gas gradually caught on, with the help of celebrity chefs like Alexis Soyer – a French author of popular cookbooks. Stateside, home economists like Sarah Tyson Rorer demonstrated how to cook on the new devices, and extolled the ways gas cooking could save time and money.

By the 1890s, ads ran throughout newspapers and ladies' magazines advertising not only gas stoves in general, but particular models.

In the early 1900s, gas stoves were a menace and cause for concern – at least in Baltimore. The Sun ran lists of deaths and injuries caused by what they called "the poor man's fuel." They ran a list of a dozen deaths that had happened in a year, with an implication that the city should take action. (In the back pages of the paper, they ran ads for gas stoves.)

Many people felt that the onus was on the users to be more careful. In a letter to the paper, one reader pointed out that men used gasoline in cars safely, yet women using gas for stoves experienced these explosions. Maybe it was the women's fault for not being cautious. Besides, the accidents could have happened with coal stoves anyway. Furthermore, the man pointed out, 30,000 people had been killed in Manchuria. Why was the Sun worrying about a dozen people dying from gas? The writer also mentioned the minor issue that a ban would cost the Standard Oil Company lost profits.

Despite the fact that explosions continued from time to time, gas caught on for cooking.

Starting in 1909, Baltimore began to explore the benefits of natural gas over gasoline. In 1915 the Sun wrote about the possibility of supplying the gas via a series of pipes, conveniently hidden beneath the sidewalks. The gas companies promised savings to consumers over coal or gasoline. Some readers wrote in to express concerns about fumes or explosions.

Ultimately, it seems, the natural gas lines were put in. Once electricity caught on, gas and electricity providers consolidated.

Along the way, there were recipes.

Gas & Electric companies hired home economists to teach homemakers how to use the new devices, often sold by those same companies. Icebox pies in the electric refrigerator, dinner on the stove, and bread in the oven. A machine to wash the laundry for you. You can just imagine the starry eyes of the aspirational housewife. Free time!

Leisure time wasn't the only fantasy being sold: Back to those icebox pies and gas-cooked dinners. Gas & Electric companies provided the recipes for free. You only needed their appliances in order to try them.

Well after people had learned how to use their stoves, cookbooks remained a standard promotional item for utility companies. Some still produce them to this day.

I have several B.G.E. Cookbooks in my collection and am aware of many more that I don't personally own. In the 1950s, they sponsored a cooking tv show on W.M.A.R. Each week, viewers received featured recipes in the mail. Many women collected these recipes into binders, and I now own several of these. B.G.E. also produced some fairly quality regional recipe collections, such as the 1985 "Maryland Classics" cookbook which contains Stuffed Ham, Sauerbraten, Maryland Fried Chicken, Peach Cake, and more. In the back, there is a section of microwave recipes – still teaching people to use those new appliances.

I have referred to this cookbook many times for Maryland recipes, but in this case I went searching for something to do with some squash and found this zucchini spice cake. The cookbook also contains a zucchini bread, but the spice cake is a bit more light and elaborately seasoned.

I have gotten more and more into making cakes in the last year or two. I finally feel like I have the skills to make just about any cake recipe turn out well. Which is why, when I do eventually get rid of my gas oven one day, I will sigh at having to learn a new way. But that's progress. Maybe not this year, or next year, but it will come for me. Ultimately I know I need only look for the recipes. And be grateful I can try them out safely. ❀

Zucchini Spice Cake:

3 eggs
2 Cup sugar
1 Cup oil, vegetable
1 Teaspoon salt
1 Teaspoon baking powder
1.5 Teaspoon vanilla extract
1 Teaspoon cinnamon
.25 Teaspoon nutmeg
.25 Teaspoon ground cloves
3 Cup sifted, all-purpose flour
2 Cup coarsely shredded, unpeeled zucchini
1 Cup chopped pecan
.25 Cup milk
Combine first 10 ingredients in large bowl of electric mixer.
Beat on medium speed for 2 minutes or until well blended.
Gradually fold in flour. Gently stir in zucchini, pecans,
and milk by hand. Pour into greased and floured 10-inch
tube pan. Bake at 350°F about 70 minutes. Cool in pan 15
minutes. Remove from pan and cool completely on wire
rack. Drizzle with Confectioners Sugar Glaze.

Recipe from Maryland Classics. Baltimore Gas & Electric Company. 1985.

Lemon Ice Box Pie, Mrs. Harry C. Michael

Posted on June 18, 2023

Next time you drop a few ice cubes into a cold beverage think of this: many early-20th-century consumers would be wary of your "artificial" ice. Unless of course, your ice happens to be harvested from a lake or a mountain somewhere.

The technology to create ice from water was first developed in the mid-1800s, but it caught on slowly. The ice trade continued to collect ice from natural stores and ship it around the country.

It's no surprise that manufactured ice might scare consumers. Think of how strange it must have seemed. As always, industry had to sway the public. The Maryland Ice Company took out an ad in the Baltimore Sun in 1892 declaring that "manufactured ice is not only purer, but will last longer and produce equally as much cold as 'natural ice.'"

Apparently, this was still a concern in 1923 when an American Ice company ad in the Evening Sun explained to readers that "American Ice is... made from filtered water and frozen in sanitary plants," and that it was "very real, absolutely pure Ice." The ad stated that American Ice had nine plants in Baltimore "all making clean, pure, healthful ice."

Whether you preferred "natural" ice or trusted newfangled manufactured ice, you had to keep it somewhere. Enter the icebox.

An added bonus of the kitchen icebox was the ability to make a pie that required little or no cooking in a sweltering kitchen, and which was refreshing when served.

The advent of home refrigerators only boosted the profile of the "ice box pie" even more – but the evocative name stuck.

Mrs. Harry C. Michael went with a classic pie flavor when she submitted this Lemon Ice Box Pie recipe to "Maryland's Famous Receipts," a 1952 cookbook produced by the Women's Auxiliary of the Rosewood School. I couldn't find out much about

Mrs. Michael. I only know she was an eclectic cook. Her other recipes in the book were for: Creamed Chicken Alexis, Oysters & Spaghetti, Veal Chops En Casserole, Peach Ice Cream, and Pumpkin Pie.

Nowadays, we might think twice before eating a block of ice from the nearest cold locale. This is one time we are not likely to see a return to "all natural." The ice box pie remains popular, especially in places where the temperatures demand a cool treat to sweeten a summer's day. ❁

Lemon Ice Box Pie

3 eggs
.5 Cup + 1 Tablespoon sugar
1 lemon
.5 Pint whipped cream
1 box vanilla wafers
Instructions:
3 egg yolks – beaten light
1/2 c. sugar
1/4 c. lemon juice – grated rind
Cook until thick in double boiler. Beat 3 egg whites, add 1 T. sugar – 1/2 pt. whipped cream. Add to the cooled custard. Crush 1 box vanilla wafers – put 1/2 on bottom of ice tray and pour in above mixture – put rest of crumbs on top. Freeze – not too hard.

Recipe from Maryland's Famous Receipts, The Woman's Auxiliary of the Rosewood State Training School. Owings Mills, MD. 1952.

Bernice Watson's Coconut Cake

Posted on February 2, 2024

Mrs. Edward Z. Watson "disclaim[ed] any fame as a cook," said a profile in the Afro-American in 1958. The article described the vivacious teacher, seamstress, and mother of two as a "party girl," who "not only adore[d] going to parties but [was] not adverse to giving them either!"

They shared her cake recipe using "many of the newest methods," including a MixMaster mixer. The title of the feature was "Mrs. Edward Watson makes the highest cake you've ever seen."

The light and fluffy cake could be served a variety of ways. "For the chocolate frosting I use the recipe right on the Hershey can," Watson declared. She also confessed to using ready-mix caramel icing. But Bernice Watson's cake is no lazy feat. With egg whites beaten separately and folded into the batter, plus a seven-minute icing made over a double boiler, the cake requires plenty of attention and generates a fair amount of dirty dishes.

I just had to make it – particularly the coconut variation, which Watson would flavor with "lemon or almond" flavoring. (I used the latter.) I couldn't find the canned style of coconut that she preferred, and I'm not skilled at cooked icings, but the recipe did indeed turn out a tall, light delightful cake.

"Sometimes I scarcely think it's worthwhile. A big beautiful cake now. A few hours, no cake at all," Watson sighed in 1958.

She was born Bernice Calverta Francis in Philadelphia in 1922, the granddaughter of a Sharp Street Methodist reverend, McHenry Jeremiah Naylor. After attending high school in Baltimore, and Coppin State Teacher's College, she went into teaching at Baltimore City Public Schools.

Along the way, she married fellow teacher Edward Z. Watson, who would serve a full career at BCPS as a teacher and later as an administrator.

Bernice took a more varied path, leaving teaching to pursue her passions as a seamstress and a designer. From 1976-1986, she worked as a librarian at the Enoch Pratt Free Library.

In the Pratt Library's African-American Department, within a special collection, "African American Funeral Programs," are the funeral programs for both Bernice and Edward Watson.

They offer a more intimate view of the lives and personalities of this couple, and their importance within their families, communities and churches. Edward's 2001 obituary describes how he worked on the B&O Railroad and at country clubs before going into teaching, and continued to hold summer and evening jobs because "he was determined to provide many advantages and opportunities" for his three children.

Both Bernice and Edward are portrayed as fun-loving. Bernice "was known for her savvy way of dressing and her great ability to design 'runway' fashions for herself and others."

Bernice C. Francis Watson's photograph on the front of her 2006 funeral program shows a woman with the same smile seen nearly fifty years earlier in her photo in the Afro-American, where she leaned over with a plate of food, dressed in a strapless white dress and statement earrings. Even her haircut remained similar later in life.

The years between were filled with social and charitable clubs, community service, children and grandchildren. No doubt they were also filled with the parties that Bernice professed her love for, and many impossibly tall and light cakes. ❀

Coconut Cake

5 Lb butter
2 Cups sugar
6 eggs
1 Teaspoon salt
1 Cup milk
4 Teaspoons baking powder
4 Cups cake flour
almond extract

Preheat oven to 350°. Grease and flour three round nine-inch cake pans. Separate egg whites from yolks. Beat egg whites until they begin to stiffen and set aside.

Cream butter until smooth. Gradually add sugar, beating well. Add egg yolks one at a time, beating well after each addition.

Sift together flour, baking powder, and salt (if using unsalted butter). Add dry ingredients to cake batter, alternating with milk, starting and ending with the flour. Stir in flavoring. Gently fold in beaten egg whites and divide among the cake pans. Bake for 25–30 minutes or until set in middle and golden brown. Fill with coconut seven-minute icing.

Seven-Minute Icing:
2 egg whites (may add yolks to cake)
.5 Cup sugar
.333 Cup water
dash salt
2 Teaspoons white corn syrup
1 Teaspoon vanilla extract
1 lb moist shredded coconut

Combine egg whites, sugar, water, salt and corn syrup over a double boiler. With water boiling below, beat rapidly until it begins to thicken, scraping the sides of the bowl frequently. Stir in vanilla and coconut. This will make a filling and topping for the cake but it isnt enough to ice the sides. If full coverage is desired, double the recipe.

Recipe adapted from the Afro-American newspaper, June 14, 1958

MRS. EDWARD Z. WATSON

Afro-American, 1958

Enoch Pratt Free Library

Jenny Lind Cakes, Emily Niernsee Cookbook

Posted on December 5, 2018

Baltimore's Front Street Theatre had undergone "extensive alterations and improvements" in 1850. Carpenters Carnan & Eckert built out a parquet for standing room theatergoers. "Skillful" painter John Delpher was hired to apply a fresh coat of paint. New curtains were hung, and 600 cushioned seats with spring-backs were installed.

A decade and a half later, Abraham Lincoln would be nominated as the republican presidential candidate in "the old Front Street Theatre"; through the years the theater was scene of the occasional theft or shooting. Those events would fade from memory long before that of the concerts that necessitated the 1850 renovations.

Hundreds of Baltimore citizens gathered in the rain on Monday December 9th, 1850 for a chance at tickets to see Jenny Lind, "The Swedish Nightingale," live in concert. Front row tickets went for the modern equivalent of a few thousand dollars. Many would-be concertgoers were dismayed that many of the remaining tickets – about 1900 in all, were quickly bought up for resale.

For the next few days, ads appeared in the Baltimore Sun, offering tickets to see Jenny Lind. Businesses that didn't have tickets to sell advertised hats to wear to the concert, "Jenny Lind Bouquets" for the concert, "Jenny Lind Candy" bearing "a perfect likeness of the divine songstress."

While it is true that P.T. Barnum did much to promote the fervor over Lind's American tour, the singer was not unknown in the U.S. before his efforts.

Would-be fans could read in the newspapers about the success of Lind's European concerts, purchase sheet music of her songs, and even buy fabric and hats named after the singer. In 1848, the Front Street Theater hosted a comic play called "Jenny Lind at Last." Across town, more "questionable skits" about Jenny Lind were performed at the Howard Street Theater.

As Lind embarked on her tour of the U.S. in 1850, fans could closely follow her travels in the news. By the time Jenny Lind arrived in Baltimore in December, "mob town" had been worked into a characteristic lather. According to Lind's biographer:

"In anticipation of her advent, some two or three thousand persons had gathered in Canton Avenue, from Broadway to the President Street Depot, with the view of obtaining a sight of her. These clustered in dense throngs around the [train] cars on their arrival... She was then driven off to the City Hotel. Here also an immense crowd had assembled, and at length, to their repeated cries for her presence, she appeared at an upper window, bowed her thanks and waved her handkerchief to those assembled, (in the rain and mud,) and then retired.

Towards the evening, the weather gradually cleared off, and about eleven o'clock, a band of musicians proceeded to the Hotel, for the purpose of serenading her. On this occasion the crowd was even larger than it had been in the morning, and at the close of the serenade she was again vociferously called for, and once more appeared. While standing at the balcony, bowing to the loud and enthusiastic applause of the multitude, she had the misfortune to drop her shawl – I say the misfortune, as she never saw the shawl again. In less than a minute it was torn into fragments, which were distributed to all who were standing near enough, to be preserved as a slight memorial of the songstress." – *"Jenny Lind in America,"* C. G. Rosenberg, 1851

"Lind-mania" reached a fever pitch thanks to P.T. Barnum's promotion of Jenny Lind's voice and her virtuous character, but 1850's crowds were primed for this kind of excitement. This was an era when people got into riots at Shakespearean Plays.

"People enjoyed opera in English for its entertainment value, not as a vehicle for self-enhancement or 'classical' improvement. Favorite airs and overtures found their way into brass-band concerts, amateur piano playing at home, and music boxes. Melodramas featured parodies of operatic plots and music. From a production standpoint, opera was big business, attracting far larger and more diverse audiences than did formal symphonic concerts of the time or, for that

matter, opera today.

The star system drove the passion for opera to a near frenzy, as audiences clamored for big-name singers.

It played havoc with local actors and musicians, who were at the mercy of touring star performers' irregular schedules, limited rehearsal time, and repertory choices.

Local managers also disliked this arrangement, but the public supported it wildly, eager to see exotic actors and singers whose reputations in some cases were well earned and in others rested entirely on hired clappers, exaggerated handbills, and contrived newspaper 'puffs.'" – "Musical Maryland," David K. Hildebrand and Elizabeth M. Schaaf, 2017

When Lind performed her Front Street Theatre concerts, the amphitheater was packed, and people crowded outside, "anxious to catch the stray notes which the power of her voice might project beyond the walls of the theater."

The Sun gushed that the "most brilliant audience [they] had ever witnessed" was "electrified by her astonishing powers as a vocalist" and "winning expression of kindness and good nature."

The lyrics "Come hither, come hither, my pretty bird, Huah, huah, huah, huah, huah" were executed "in a style so novel, so difficult, and withal so enchanting, that it defies adequate description," the Sun reported.

Of course, not everyone appreciated the ubiquity of Jenny Lind.

In the Cecil Whig, a correspondent from "Lindiana" reported that "we had yesterday the pleasure of being shaved with a Jenny Lind razor, by a Jenny Lind Barber, scented with Jenny Lind cologne... put on a Jenny Lind hat, walked into a Jenny Lind restaurant, partook of Jenny Lind sausages..." and on and on until they "fell into a profound Jenny Lind reverie."

Many of my cookbook manuscript authoresses were at least taken enough with Jenny Lind to save the recipe for "Jenny Lind Cakes." Emily Niernsee, whose cookbook is in the collections at the Maryland Historical Society, used baking soda and cream of tartar to leaven her cakes, and flavored them with vanilla. These modern choices persuaded me to use her recipe.

The results, which I baked in a muffin pan, were pleasant and not too sweet.

The legacy of the Front Street Theatre ultimately came to a tragic end. In December 1895 a panic over a false fire alarm became known as the "Front Street Theatre Disaster" when at least 23 people were trampled to death. The building was razed in 1904.

Despite this, Jenny Lind's concerts lingered in the Baltimore memory for decades to come, with readers writing letters reminiscing about the monumental event, or sharing photos of their saved ticket stubs and programs. One man wrote of how he'd arrived at the theater to find the concert sold out. With two gold pieces in his pocket, he bribed the door man to get in. "He said afterward that if he had had to pay $100 to hear Jennie Ling sing he would have considered it worth the money."

As Jenny Lind was ushered covertly to her train for Washington DC, the Baltimore Sun recalled, (apocryphally), she "expressed herself as better pleased with Baltimore and its people than any American city she had visited." ❋

Jenny Lind Cakes

"Stir a coffee cup of butter with one pound of pulverized sugar – add the yolks of 6 eggs well beaten – 1 teaspoon of soda dissolved in a cup of milk, 2 teaspoons of cream tartar in four(4) cups flour. Beat the whites very light and add alternately with the flour. Flavor with lemon or vanilla."

From the Emily [Bradenbaugh] Niernsee's cookbook (1861), John R. Niernsee Papers, Maryland Historical Society Special Collections MS2457

Clam Fritters Virginia Roeder

Posted on September 16, 2017

Home Economics as a professional pursuit codified "women's work" and amended school curricula, but it also opened doors for women professionally.

The name Virginia Roeder may ring a bell to longtime Baltimore recipe collectors. For 23 years she wrote for the "women's pages" of the Baltimore Evening Sun, offering guidance on cooking and housekeeping. She penned three columns weekly, totaling around 3500 over the course of her career. The most enduring legacy of these columns is the "Fun with Food" and "Fun with Sea Food" cookbooks still serving many Baltimore kitchens today.

In 1953, the Sun profiled Roeder, who was then hosting a Television show called "Nancy Troy's Food Show." (I am not sure why she assumed the "role" of Nancy Troy on the show.) The Sun reported that Roeder's days began at 5:30 a.m., preparing breakfast for her husband and three children before heading to work at the William S. Baer School where she taught home economics to disabled children. After a day's work she prepared dinner for her family and then "[sat] down with her husband to bring his company's books up to date" for his wholesale distribution business.

In 1961 the Sun ran a highly illustrated tour of the Roeder's home on Meadowwood Road, asking "how does an advisor to housewives manage her own home?" They described the decor in the "immaculate" home, complete with pool table, children's playroom, "roomy pink kitchen," and a corner desk in the master bedroom where Roeder typed her columns on Saturdays.

Born Virginia Voigt in Oklahoma, Roeder followed in her mother's footsteps to pursue a career in education, earning a bachelor's degree from the University of Science and Arts at Oklahoma (formerly Oklahoma College for Women). She soon ended up in Baltimore, where she made her mark on the school system, the food culture, and even in banking.

She's been inducted to the Oklahoma College for Women hall of fame, where a biography of her achievements declares itself to be "simply a list of firsts." In addition to earning a master's and a doctoral degree at Johns Hopkins, Virginia Roeder became the "first female Deputy Superintendent, Baltimore City Public Schools," "first woman president, Maryland Association of Secondary School Principals," and "first woman board of directors, Carrolton Bank."

After retiring from education she continued to be a successful businesswoman in real estate and travel agencies.

Even while working towards all of these goals, Roeder maintained the refined image of an ideal mid-century "housewife."

I got my copies of "Fun with Sea Food" from the Book Thing. The photo at the front shows a smiling Virginia Roeder. The author's biography lists one accomplishment after another before declaring "Mrs. Roeder does all the cooking for her family."

Two recipes for crab cakes are included, one of which has been marked "excellent" by my book's previous owner. Other sections besides "The Delightful Crab" are adorably titled: "The Fascinating Fish," "The Sophisticated Scallop," "The Admirable Oyster."

The recipe for Clam Fritters asks below the title, "Haven't you ever made them?" I hadn't so I took Virginia Roeder up on her challenge. ❁

Clam Fritters

.5 Pint clams, minced
.75 Cups flour
.5 Tablespoons baking powder
1 teaspoon crab seasoning (adapted – Roeder used nutmeg and salt.)
1 beaten egg
.5 Cups milk
2 Teaspoons grated onion
.5 Tablespoons melted butter
oil for frying
Sift dry ingredients together. Combine egg, milk, onion, butter and clams. Add to dry ingredients and stir until smooth. Drop batter by teaspoonfuls into hot oil, 350 degrees, and fry until golden brown on each side.
Recipe adapted from "Fun With Sea Food," Virginia Roeder

Old-Fashioned Citron Preserves, Agnes M. Poist

Posted on August 14, 2022

"It has no flavour, very little sweetness, and doubtful nutritional value."

– Bob Wildfong, executive director, Seeds of Diversity

The Sisson Street Community Garden has become a sacred place to me. Some fifty neighbors and I put our tastes out on display, in neat little delineated squares, some (me) in unkempt chaos, others with towering beanpoles, and many burdened tomato cages. The crops are as varied as the methods: colorful peppers, luscious greens, beastly zucchini vines, and of course all manner of tomatoes. All summer long, our motley patch of vegetables soaks in the ample sun from behind the gas station.

In 2021 I decided to use my space to grow Citron Melons.

My database contains a few dozen recipes for preserving the confusingly-named watermelon relative, but the actual melons are nowhere to be found in a Maryland farmer's market. The only way to get them is to grow them from seed, or to know someone who does (intentionally or not – in warmer climates they grow wild in fields and pastures.)

Citrons are basically like watermelon minus the good part. Native to the Kalahari Desert in Africa, they are in fact related to watermelons – and are a possible ancestor. Unlike watermelons, they're not especially palatable, but used to be widely grown for preserving. Due to their thick rinds, the melons can be stored (typically packed in straw in a cool place) for months on end. They are also full of pectin and can be combined with other fruits to extend their flavor in preserves. Their frequent pairings with citrus fruit may be the reason for their confusing name.

Because of that name, it is kind of hard to research citron and its uses, but most old recipes are essentially the same thing as watermelon rind preserves. A 1928 newspaper article indicated citron melon explicitly as one of the "best ingredients" for fruit cakes. By the time that piece was written, the melons had already become hard to find. "It is worth hunting for," the author suggested.

As the fall approached and I finally amassed enough melons to follow a recipe with, they began to disappear. I sighed. I assumed someone mistook my Citrons for watermelons. Well, I thought, they will be disappointed. Yet the melons continued to disappear one by one and I grew irritated and dejected.

I resigned myself to grow them another year, perhaps in multiple locations, and I took a sample melon and cut it open, inspecting and photographing the white interior with its bright red seeds.

Eventually, I learned through the garden grapevine that mine and other gourds that had been pilfered never made it to anyone's dinner table. It turned out that some of the kids who play in the park had been using them for projectiles to lob at one another. I had to laugh.

2022 went more smoothly and provided me with an ample crop of Citron Melons to work with. And so, finally, I flipped through my recipes and made some choices. Pickled Citron, Citron Preserve – and then there's the host of recipes that could be referring to "real" citrons, the lemon relative. Citron Cake, Citron Ice, Citron Meringue. Those are out.

I knew I'd be working with a fairly historic recipe. Citron Melon was a mainstay in old recipe manuscripts. Mary Randolph suggested using it to make a flavored ice dessert in the 1824 "Virginia Housewife." A recipe appeared in Elizabeth Ellicott Lea's 1859 "Domestic Cookery" flavored with lemon, mace, and ginger. Maryland cookbooks for the next several decades invariably included a recipe or two for some type of citron melon preserve or pickle.

Ultimately, it was a newspaper recipe that got my attention.

Mrs. Agnes M. Poist of Laurel Maryland won third place in the 1911 Baltimore Sun recipe contest with her recipe for "Old-Fashioned Citron Preserve." Mrs. Poist didn't bother with false modesty. "Anything more delicious than this recipe for preserved citron could hardly be found," she wrote. "Everyone who has tasted it pronounces it first class. It has also taken first prize at a county fair."

Mrs. Poist was born in 1877 to children of German immigrants, Mary E. and John A. Hohman. From 1897 until his death in 1914, John operated Hohman's Cafe at 868 North Howard Street, across from Richmond Market, and near the Fifth Regiment Armory. The block was demolished and replaced with Maryland General Hospital, but the Richmond Market building is still visibly incorporated into the hospital complex.

After John's death, his son, Agnes' brother Henry, took over the business in some form. Henry is listed as a "confectioner" at the address in the 1930 census, and later in life he was a salesman of baking supplies.

Agnes M. was given the birth name Mary Agnes Hohman. She became Mrs. William A Poist in 1899 when she married Poist, who was a superintendent of street cleaning.

Agnes' wedding attire was described in great detail in the Sun:

"The bride was gowned in grey novelty cloth, trimmed with cut steele and mousseline de sole. A picture hat of white plumes and chiffon and grey silk gloves completed her costume. She carried a bunch of white sweet peas."

Agnes died in 1960 and is buried in Laurel with her husband.

The Hohmans were a fairly prominent family due to the cafe being a popular meeting spot for locals, but also apparently due to John A. Hohman's personality. In 1911 the Sun wrote, "not only is Mr. Hohman exceedingly well-liked by the market people and those who live near his place, but every one of the older members of the Fifth Regiment holds him in deep regard. Many happy little parties have been held by the different companies in his dining room and the Duke [as Mr. Hohman is called in the article] always smiled on the festivities with a blandness that begot good cheer. Mr. Hohman congratulates himself daily on the fact that he resembles Grover Cleveland. Everybody who ever saw the late President agrees with him that he is practically a living double."

Speaking of blandness, I was pretty disappointed when the preserves cooled down and I took a taste. After all that work seeding and cutting the melon (though not into the 'fancy shapes' suggested by Agnes; I only have so much time) I found the sweet and faintly citrusy cube that I bit into didn't exactly thrill me. And I'd made a gallon of this stuff.

I put it in the fridge and bit into some of my remaining pieces of candied ginger, a shortcut I'd resorted to after I'd burned the ginger in the pan.

A few days later, I pulled a jar out of the fridge and, with some resignation, I ladled the chunks and syrup onto some yogurt.

The fridge had worked some magic. The citrus flavor seemed somehow brighter, the ginger came back, and best of all, the cubes had turned into alluring pieces of shiny sweet glass. Refreshingly cool, they resembled the sensation of lychee jelly candy.

I don't know that I'll grow the melons again, especially considering their appeal to curious children as a weapon in play. I'm glad I finally got my own taste of the Citron Melon, another formerly common garden crop that has become a lost curiosity.

Old-Fashioned Citron Preserve

"Anything more delicious than this recipe for preserved citron could hardly be found. Everyone who has tasted it pronounces it first-class. It has also taken first price at a county fair. To 6 pounds of citron use 4 1/2 pounds of sugar, 4 lemons, 3 seedless oranges and 1/4 pound of ginger root. Slice the lemons and oranges and boil them in 2 quarters of water until they look clear. Save the water they are boiled in, removing them from it into a dish of cold water, where they may stand over night. In the morning scrape the ginger root, slice it into three parts of water and boil it in the water 1 hour. Add to the ginger water the water the lemons and oranges were cooked in and the sugar, stirring till it is melted. Skim this syrup well. When the syrup is clear drop in the citron, slices of lemons and oranges. Cook till the citron is transparent. These preserves are excellent to serve with ice-cream or around an iced pudding. Cut the citron in fancy shapes."

Recipe from Baltimore Sun 1911 recipe contest, contributed by Mrs. Agnes Poist

Corn Pone from "The Chesapeake Collection"

Posted on March 21, 2019

Maryland cooking (like that of many places that were/are dining destinations), has two sides to it. Front and center we have the legacy represented by the hotels and caterers - the terrapin, the deviled crab, the fine wines from around the world straight from the Port of Baltimore. On the back end are the legions of home cooks who worked with limited resources but far more flexibility to put white potato pies, stuffed ham, and scrapple -plus a given assortment of heritage foods- on the tables of their family and friends.

The blurred lines and exchanges between the two are too complex to get into, but one thing is certain: we are blessed with pretty good documentation of the recipes and preferences of the home cooks.

Interestingly, it is the historically limited roles of women that we have to thank for this. Since the end of the 19th century, when women wanted to raise money for a cause, the most popular course of action was to produce a community cookbook. As times changed, so did the cookbooks - incorporating more business and design resources, and recipes from all kinds of cooks.

I don't have a point of comparison, but either way, Marylanders (mostly women) have produced an astounding number of impressive cookbooks. To stand out among them is a bit of a feat.

The 1983 cookbook "The Chesapeake Collection," by the Woman's Club of Denton is one of those standouts. The Woman's Club was founded in 1919, and had engaged in a range of activities from providing soup & clothing to the needy to securing a nurse for Caroline County in the 1920s. The club also had a hand in the founding of the local volunteer fire department and public library.

The purpose of The Chesapeake Collection was to raise funds to restore the clubs headquarters, an 1883 schoolhouse that was in a pretty dire state of disrepair.

The book, as the many Maryland newspapers that covered it were sure to mention, was "marketed nationally" and published in Tennessee. Although I didn't find many references to The Chesapeake Collection in digitized newspapers farther away than Ohio, the Maryland papers alone surely generated a lot of interest. The book sold 15,000 copies in its first two printings.

The Chesapeake Collection's runaway success allowed the club to seek out another beneficiary in 1984. They settled on the Chesapeake Bay Foundation. The logic was that the book had preserved the recipes, and its sales had allowed the Woman's Club to preserve the schoolhouse. Supporting preservation of the Bay ecosystem was an ideal next step, according to club president Beth Adams.

Successful marketing campaign aside, the Woman's Club had created a high-quality community cookbook, with original photos, artwork, and a well-curated range of recipes.

In the Easton Star-Democrat, Mary Siemer wrote that some of the recipes were older than the historic schoolhouse that the club was restoring, "so they must be good." Old Line Plate readers are invited to have a little chuckle at that assumption.

Nonetheless, The Chesapeake Collection is indeed filled with tempting fare.

Among the recipes sourced from people outside of club members are a crabcake recipe from then-Governor Harry Hughes, who passed away on March 13th, 2019. There's a chicken recipe from Frank Perdue. Several restaurants shared recipes, including the Tidewater Inn's crab imperial and 'Oysters A La Gino' from the Robert Morris Inn.

Theres a stuffed ham recipe from Roy Dyson, who won a seat in congress after Robert Bauman's scandal.

One of the most notable sections of the book, aside of course from the seafood recipes, is the game section, which contains many recipes for waterfowl alongside muskrat, squirrel pot pie, and more surprisingly, "Choptank Frog Legs."

The recipe I made, for a corn pone, was contributed by Regina

Mueller (1910-1998.)

Mueller was a member of the Woman's Club's "bell-ringing committee," in charge of deciding when and how many times to ring the bell at the old schoolhouse that the club used as a headquarters. In 1983, on the centennial of the building of the schoolhouse, the bell was rung 100 times. In 1987 it was rung to honor the 353rd anniversary of the Ark & the Dove reaching Maryland. The newspapers never mentioned how many times the bell rang on that day, but I am sure the committee settled on an appropriate number of rings. ✻

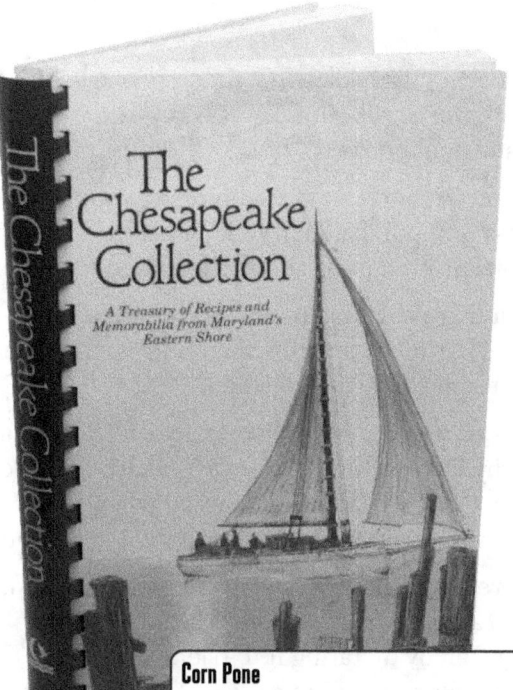

Corn Pone

1 Cup flour
1 Teaspoon salt
1 Teaspoon baking soda
3 Tablespoon sugar
1 Cup cornmeal
3 Tablespoon melted bacon fat
2 Cup yogurt

Preheat a skillet or cookie sheet in oven at 400°. Sift together flour, salt, sugar, and baking soda. Stir in corn meal, then yogurt and melted bacon grease. Pour into pan. Bake 35 minutes or until golden on top.

Recipe from "The Chesapeake Collection: A Treasury of Recipes and Memorabilia from Maryland's Eastern Shore" by the Woman's Club of Denton

French Rolls Elizabeth Ellicott Lea

Posted on July 13, 2016

Though I've referenced her book a few times, I have been a bit neglectful in discussing Elizabeth Ellicott Lea, author of one of the oldest Maryland cookbooks.

"Domestic cookery; useful receipts, and hints to young housekeepers" was first published in 1845, with several augmented editions printed in Baltimore in subsequent decades.

In addition to famously providing us the first printed recipe for scrapple, Lea offers her take on some Maryland classics such as terrapin soup, oyster pie and fried chicken.

Elizabeth Ellicott Lea was born in Ellicott City in 1793 into a notable and wealthy Quaker family. Her father, George Ellicott, owned mills on the Patapsco which processed wheat and corn. The historic home she was born in remains intact in Ellicott City.

As an adult, she lived a rural life in Delaware and Maryland, finally settling into a home called Walnut Hill where she wrote the book – often by dictating it to friends while she was bedridden with an unknown illness.

Historian William Woys Weaver has presented his research on Lea in a reprinted edition of "Domestic Cookery" that was published in 1983. Those familiar with Weaver's work will know that this left me no stones to turn. I can only quote and paraphrase his own words.

"Though her recipes may seem overly plain by today's standards, rural eating habits before the Civil War were generally simple. Practicality, economy, and simplicity at the table were not new themes in American culinary literature during this period. But in Quaker terms, nothing is as complex as simplicity." – William Woys Weaver, "A Quaker Woman's Cookbook"

Weaver points out that Lea, through her family connections, had a wide social network at her disposal. The recipes and ingredients in her book, intended as a useful guide to her daughter Mary Lea Stabler, and to other newly wedded women, reflects a larger range of influence than the cookery books of other Quaker women. According to Weaver, correspondence between Lea and her daughter "give glimpses into the role food played in the complex world of cousins and other relatives, who thought nothing of sending each other large quantities of produce, meats, or even live lemon trees."

"The most obvious foods of native origin in 'Domestic Cookery' are beans and poke; green corn soup; several squash dishes; terrapin (without the wine and seasonings); all of the pumpkin recipes with the exception of pumpkin preserve; and a number of cornmeal dishes, including some breads and puddings." – William Woys Weaver, "A Quaker Woman's Cookbook"

In addition to the recipes, the book contains a percentage of helpful household hints (lifehacks?) that is higher than in my other 19th century cook books. Lea shares folk remedies for ailments ranging from coughs and headaches to a "remarkable" cure for deafness. (There is no miracle lost to time – the patient simply had a massive wax buildup which was loosened with a warm compress). Also included in the book are dyes, polishes, cleaning solutions, instructions for crafting beds and candles, as well as advice on managing servants, raising compassionate children, and more. Also stressed is the importance of charity, with practical suggestions about saving food for the poor, served with a watchword:

One eminent for his charities, near the close of his life, made this remark: 'What I spent I lost, but what I gave away remains with me.'

I've been gradually getting to "know" Elizabeth Ellicott Lea a little better, and coming to really like her.

At first her no-frills thrift seemed unexciting and maybe even a little stern. Certainly she doesn't radiate the Maryland pride of other authors who boast their Maryland-ness in the titles of their cookbooks. Lea was a Quaker first and foremost, and a Marylander by chance. But thrift as an ethos suits me well, and more and more I've come to trust Lea with what to do with seasonal ingredients and simple comforts, like home-baked bread.

I recently chose her recipe for "French Rolls" to make some grilled sandwiches with.

I'm no bread expert, so I'm not sure what makes these rolls "French." A recipe in the Maryland Gazette in 1831 -14 years before Lea's book- bears little resemblance to Lea's method.

Lea offers ample general advice on baking bread, "the most important article of food" by her estimation.

"It is significant to note that within the context of the broader regional culture in which Elizabeth Lea lived, there was a large class of poor whites and blacks who depended upon hearth baking [in a dutch oven] as their sole source of bread. It is interesting that Lea's recipe took this into account, because very few period cookbooks, American or British, devote much space to it. "Baking in dirt," as some Welsh cooks characterize it (the pot is covered with ashes), was generally considered primitive by the 1840s and an unappetizing way to go about the business of bread baking, regardless of the delightful 'hearthy' flavor." – William Woys Weaver, "A Quaker Woman's Cookbook: The "Domestic Cookery" of Elizabeth Ellicott Lea"

Lea's tips on rising, testing stove heat, using a dutch oven or a brick oven, etc. may be somewhat useful to a hearth cook but I can't say for sure what her yeast would've been like. The 1831 recipe in the Gazette suggested 'distillers yeast' or 'ale yeast', brewing being just as common an activity as baking. Lea has advice on making the yeast from hops, corn flour, potatoes, or milk. Hop yeast is declared best.

I also can't claim to know what her flour would have been like. Let's be real here – Maryland is corn country. Although once home to many mills, the types of wheat that grow well in Maryland are not what we would pass off as bread flour today. According to Lynne Hoot from The Maryland Grain Producers Association, "Maryland grows soft red winter wheat which is not a good bread flour, it is used more for cookies, pretzels and pastry."

This may have differed slightly in the past, as flour had not been industrialized to the uniform consistency we now know.

"Millers produced a variety of flours depending upon the moisture in the grain, its quality, starch and gluten content, and the fineness of

the grinding. Typically the miller blended various types of wheat to produce a particular product. Mills yielded several grades of flour. The best or most pure was the pastry white, followed by white, then seconds, thirds, and middlings. The bran, which was the husk of the grain, and the pollard, or the part of the wheat next to the husk, were discarded or fed to animals." – Tillers of the Soil: A History of Agriculture in Mid-Maryland, Paula S. Reed, 2011

Maryland was home to dozens of grist mills, and millers created their own blends that varied from mill to mill.

Before transportation brought in large-scale competition from the midwest, Maryland's rivers were dotted with mills, including Elizabeth Lea's family's mill. Many ruins remain along the banks of the Patapsco, or have been reduced to the innumerable algae-covered bricks that can be found in the riverbed.

"Most of our wheat for harvest is double cropped with soybeans so we get 3 crops in 2 years. Corn, winter wheat, short season soybeans, a cover crop and then year 2, back to corn. Our production acreage is about 250,000 acres and about 18 million bushels. We grow a lot more wheat as a cover crop but that is not harvested, it is simply used for environmental protection to take up any remaining nutrients left from the previous crop (and mineralized from crop residue left on the field), and to protect the soil from erosion." – Lynne Hoot from The Maryland Grain Producers Association

Curious how the most uncompromising of local-food evangelists deal with this, I reached out to Woodberry Kitchen. Much like in Lea's time, the bakers compensate with blends that vary based on what is available.

"We are indeed using quite a bit of local flour, thanks to the incredible work of a few farmers. Heinz Thomet at Next Step Produce in Charles County, MD is growing a number of varieties of wheat, as well as barley, rye, sorghum, buckwheat, and rice. He has a German made Haussler 20" stone mill that he uses to mill flour for us. Omar Beiler in Kinzer, PA is the other significant source of flour for us. He grows heritage varieties of wheat, as well as emmer, einkorn, and some heritage varieties of corn. We get our corn products from him, as well as our whole wheat flour and a "T-85" or high extraction flour. He has an Austrian made Ostiroller 20" stone mill. Our last local source is Small Valley Milling; they specialize in spelt and we get our whole

and white spelt flours from them." – Russell Trimmer, bread baker at Woodberry Kitchen

Luckily for the buying public, their spelt bread is -bafflingly- not gross.

this type of baking requires a level of intuition that is hard to comprehend in the age of industrialized flour. But according to some, we have been paying a price for consistency.

"Before the advent of industrial agriculture, Americans enjoyed a wide range of regional flours milled from equally diverse wheats, which in turn could be used to make breads that were astonishingly flavorful and nutritious. For nearly a century, however, America has grown wheat tailored to an industrial system designed to produce nutrient-poor flour and insipid, spongy breads soaked in preservatives. For the sake of profit and expediency, we forfeited pleasure and health" – Ferris Jabr, "Bread Is Broken" New York Times 2015

Lea advises that "coarse brown flour or middlings makes very sweet light bread, by putting in scalded corn meal, say, to two loaves, half a pint, and is also good to use for breakfast made as buckwheat cakes..." For some recipes she recommends saleratus, a baking-soda precursor.

Her french rolls recipe (as I attempted it) turned out lovely, and took relatively little effort. Most importantly, it helped us get further acquainted when she asserted "there is nothing in any department of cooking that gives more satisfaction to a young housekeeper than to have accomplished what is called good baking." ✳

French Rolls

"To one quart of sweet milk, boiled and cooled, half a pound of butter, half a tea-cup of yeast, a little salt, and flour enough to make a soft dough; beat up the milk, butter and yeast in the middle of the flour; let it stand till light, in a warm place; then work it up with the whites of two eggs, beaten light; let it rise again, then mould out into long rolls; let them stand on the board or table, to lighten, an hour or two, then grease your pans and bake in an oven or stove."

Recipe from "Domestic Cookery, Useful Receipts, and Hints to Young Housekeepers" by Elizabeth E. Lea

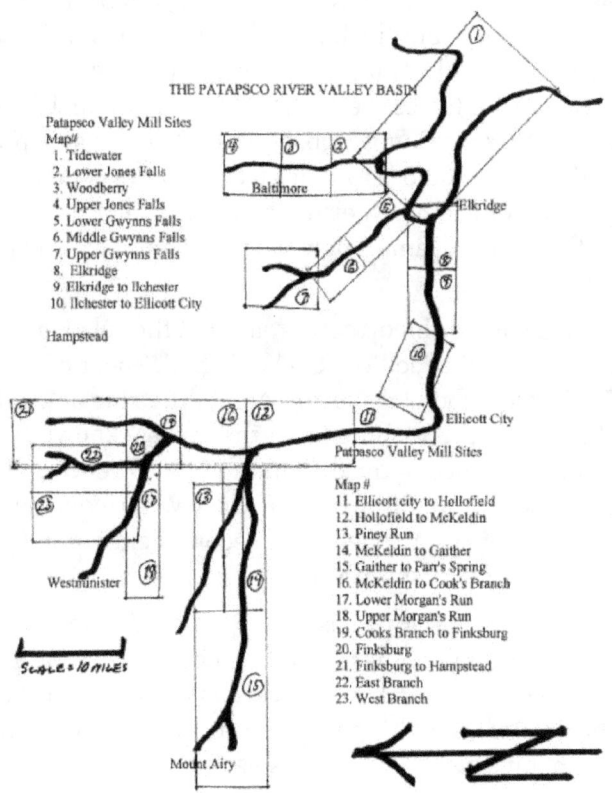

THE PATAPSCO RIVER VALLEY BASIN

Patapsco Valley Mill Sites
Map#
1. Tidewater
2. Lower Jones Falls
3. Woodberry
4. Upper Jones Falls
5. Lower Gwynns Falls
6. Middle Gwynns Falls
7. Upper Gwynns Falls
8. Elkridge
9. Elkridge to Ilchester
10. Ilchester to Ellicott City

Baltimore

Elkridge

Hampstead

Ellicott City

Patapsco Valley Mill Sites

Map #
11. Ellicott city to Hollofield
12. Hollofield to McKeldin
13. Piney Run
14. McKeldin to Gaither
15. Gaither to Parr's Spring
16. McKeldin to Cook's Branch
17. Lower Morgan's Run
18. Upper Morgan's Run
19. Cooks Branch to Finksburg
20. Finksburg
21. Finksburg to Hampstead
22. East Branch
23. West Branch

Westminister

SCALE = 10 MILES

Mount Airy

Milling regions, "A Guide to Patapsco Valley Mill Sites"

Strawberry Pretzel Salad, Dee Carney

Posted on June 16, 2019

"Strawberry Pretzel Salad" is the stuff of potluck legend. Fruit; Jell-o; creamy whipped filling; and then – surprise! – a crunchy salty bottom-crust. It requires just enough assembly to be special. It's quirky enough to be memorable. It's the kind of "Suzie Homemaker" recipe that gets frequently requested from newspapers, and that people love to claim is of their own inspired invention.

Pretzels used as a crumb crust for pies may not be as ubiquitous as graham crackers, but the idea is not unheard of. 1950s recipe columns encouraged home cooks to give pretzel crust a try. "Sounds dizzy but tastes great," the Orlando Sentinel declared in 1953. The Warren County Observer in Pennsylvania promised readers that they would "say it has a crunchiness and toasty taste that's perfect for a lemon meringue pie" in 1954. Pretzel crust lemon chiffon pie became a new twist on lemon pie and other desserts.

Many online sources incorrectly state that the salad originated with the 1963 "Joys of Jell-o" cookbook. L.M. Zoller of the "I'll Make It Myself" food blog wrote a great little zine on the topic and debunked this. L.M. noted that the earliest known (as of this writing) instance of the dish in the 1960 "Brentwood Civic Club Cookbook" from Brentwood Pennsylvania, contributed by Gerry Franz Sullivan, a daughter of second-generation German immigrants in the Pittsburgh area.

Some sources also refer to this as a "Southern" dish for whatever reason, but we won't bother with that. I believe that the layered strawberry concept may have appeared in Jell-o recipe books – but the pivotal flourish- the pretzel crust – was not included. Without that it's just a Jell-o fruit salad.

The first newspaper appearance of Strawberry Pretzel Salad that I found was in 1972, in the Chicago Tribune, as "Pretzel-Crust Strawberry Dessert," attributed to Mrs. Paul Meiners. I can't

128   Strawberry Pretzel Salad

identify Mrs. Meiners for certain, but I found a Paul Meiners in the Chicago area, the son of German immigrants.

In June 1974 the recipe appeared in the Bemidji, Minnesota Pioneer "Cooking with Candace" column under the more fetching name "Strawberry Pretzel Surprise."

In 1975, the dessert got its big break at the Florida Strawberry Festival in Plant City. Mrs. Merrill R. Stephan won the grand prize in the festival's recipe contest with Strawberry Pretzel Salad, and the recipe has been a 'women's pages' favorite ever since. Mrs. Stephan (maiden name Clara Eller) was 77 at the time she entered the contest, and Florida newspapers reported that she was surprised by the win, which earned her a new freezer.

Despite all of the glory, Clara Stephan didn't claim to have invented the recipe, admitting that she got it from her elder sister in Illinois. That sister was Katherine Pfleeger, who lived in their home state and married Jacob W. Pfleeger. Like Mr. Paul Meiners, Pfleeger's parents were German immigrants. The German community connection may explain the affinity for pretzels. For instance, one version of Pennsylvania Dutch Shoofly Pie is made with a pretzel crust.

Jacob Pfleeger died of illness in 1951, while Clara's husband Lt. Col. Merrill Stephan died in Japan in 1954. The widowed sisters each partook in various social and charity groups, and apparently traded recipes. Both women died in 1987.

That same year, Dee Carney submitted the Strawberry Pretzel Salad recipe to "Black-Eyed Susan Country," a cookbook benefitting Saint Agnes Hospital in Baltimore. Some of my cookbooks have variations on the formula, including one made with pineapple, but I wanted to go for the famous strawberry version.

It was a hit; a perfect refreshing dessert after an afternoon of hot dogs and pasta salads. Perhaps Strawberry Pretzel Salad never got famous enough for anyone to have claimed its invention, but signs point to Pennsylvania origins. Newspapers recipe columns and community cookbooks have spread the tasty treat elsewhere – perhaps to a cookout near you. ❀

Strawberry Pretzel Salad

2 Cups pretzels, coarsely crushed
3.5 Tablespoons sugar
.75 Cup melted butter
8 oz cream cheese, softened
1 Cup sugar

1 large container frozen whipped topping
2 3 oz boxes strawberry gelatin
2 cups boiling water
30 oz strawberries

Mix pretzels, 3.5 Tb sugar and melted butter and press into a 9 x 13 inch pan. Bake at 400° for 6 minutes.

Beat cream cheese and whipped topping with 1 cup sugar, spread over baked pretzel crust.

Dissolve gelatin in boiling water. Mix in berries. Jell for 20 minutes in refrigerator. Pour slowly over cream layer. Place in freezer. Allow to stand 30 minutes before serving. Serves 10 to 12.

Recipe adapted from "Black-Eyed Susan Country: A Collection of Recipes" published by the Saint Agnes Hospital Auxiliary

Clara Stephan, Tampa Tribune, 1975

Chocolate Ice Cream, Mrs. Percy Duvall

Posted on July 3, 2018

The preface for the Melwood Cookbook gives a lofty -if somewhat bewildering- purpose for the book:

"This book is compiled and published as a means of raising money with which to build a club house, in order that the aims and purposes of [the Woman's Club of Melwood District] shall be the more fully realized... for when we shall have a place of meeting, to which we shall feel free to invite others of like aim, we may find in the free discussion of existing conditions, a solution that shall result in the bettering of ourselves, our homes, and our neighborhood, known as it is as a 'Pretty fine place to live in'."

Although the book was compiled in 1920 by women from the Upper Marlboro area of Prince George's County, the overall collection of recipes gives an impression similar to late 19th century cookbooks by Southern ladies like Jane Gilmor Howard and Marietta Gibson.

The Melwood Cookbook's primary author, Mrs. Percy Duvall (née Matilda Roome) was born in 1864 in New York, but she fancied herself a "Daughter of the South." Her mother Catherine Wilcox had been from Savannah Georgia, born to a family of tobacco merchants. When the family fled north during the Civil War, Catherine met and married William Oscar Roome – a Union Army Captain. After Matilda was born, the Roomes moved from New York to northern Virginia.

Young Matilda, according to her biography in "Littell's Living Age," suffered after her mother died and her father remarried. Her stepmother, a "Long Island Yankee," made her do household chores in spite of the family having "black servants." Woe is me, poor little Matilda. Matilda escaped her tragic homelife by taking art classes and learning to paint.

Around 1890, Matilda married William Littell, a tennis friend of her brother's. In an exciting scheme to support his new wife, Will Littell signed on with Dr. Frederick Cook aboard the

Miranda – an expedition to the North Pole.

Meanwhile, Matilda put her art schooling to work. She went into business decorating lampshades and selling them to local shops in New York. The lampshades became so popular that they were shipped to stores all over the country. "Tillie" Roome Littell also began to contribute recipes and crafts to women's magazines like "Table Talk" and "The Delineator."

Unfortunately, the Miranda hit an iceberg and Will had to head home empty-handed and without glory. According to the story, he hitched a ride on a fishing boat, sleeping on a pile of fish.

Matilda wasn't too happy with her husband arriving back in New York broke and smelling like fish. Nor was Will feeling too adequate in light of his wife's financial success. The couple was divorced and Matilda went on to work as a secretary to stockbroker J. Edward Addicks, providing the man with real-estate advice that made him quite wealthy.

Eventually, Matilda invested in her own piece of real estate. Mount Airy, a Southern Maryland home built by the Calvert family, would finally allow her to live out her dreams of being the "mistress" of a Southern home. And she played the part – her biography talks of her managing sharecroppers who would be "dishonest if not supervised" ... oh brother.

Matilda's second marriage was to an Upper Marlboro neighbor, Percy Duvall, in 1908. It was during this marriage that she compiled the Melwood Cookbook.

Mrs. Duvall belonged to a large social network that allegedly included U.S. Presidents, diplomats, politicians, and businessmen. Duvall's cooking was renowned. Recipes from the cookbook frequently appeared in The Prince George's enquirer and Southern Maryland Advertiser. To bring in more income, Duvall began opening her home for meals to business travelers. She renamed the mansion Dower House to avoid confusion with Mt. Airy in Montgomery County. The popularity of Dower House led to a real-estate offer that the savvy businesswoman couldn't refuse. She sold Dower House to newspaper editor Cissy Patterson in 1931. She forever regretted it.

This ice cream recipe states that "this is the way chocolate ice cream is made in France." Matilda did indeed visit France in the early 1900s, when she went to Paris to take operatic singing lessons. Despite the recipe containing a staggering cup of flour, I followed formula. The end result tasted like a chocolate frosty! This recipe is best served directly from ice cream maker as it will freeze quite hard.

Matilda's second marriage eventually ended in divorce as well. A 1930 census lists the value of her estate as $40k and the value of Percy Duvall's at $50 dollars. At the time of his death in 1958, he was residing with his twin sister.

I couldn't figure out what became of Will Littell. There is still debate over whether the captain of the Miranda, Dr. Frederick Cook, ever actually reached the North Pole. To some, he is considered a bit of a charlatan, although he has his defenders.

Matilda died in 1964, just a few weeks shy of 100 years. Who knows whether the Melwood women ever did build their clubhouse. ❈

Chocolate Ice Cream

1 Quart rich milk
1.5 Cup sugar
1 Cup flour
.25 can cocoa (an antique cocoa can of the era appears to be 8 oz)
vanilla extract
.5 Cup butter
1 Pint cream
1 additional Pint milk, added the last thing

Bring milk to a boil, but do not allow it to boil before adding sugar and flour mixed and smoothed with the cocoa. When this is smooth, stir in the scalded milk. Allow to boil a minute, or until the milk is thickened. Remove from the fire and add the butter. When this is melted, add the vanilla and cream. If this is not sweet enough, add additional sugar and stir until dissolved. Add the cream and the additional pint of milk just before freezing. This is the way chocolate ice cream is made in France.

Recipe from The Melwood Cook Book, 1920, Women's Club Of Melwood District

Mount Airy, 1936, John O. Brostrup, loc.gov

Tilly Roome with painting, "Littell's Living Age"

Fried Sea Bass, Mabel Roberts

Posted on July 24, 2022

Sometime in the early 1900s, Mabel Roberts took a vacation to the Mount Washington Hotel in Bretton Woods, New Hampshire. She returned with recipes from a memorable meal she had enjoyed: fried Sea Bass with Remoulade sauce. She jotted them down into her "Housekeeper's Casket and Cook's Delight," a blank recipe notebook printed by the Baltimore press Cushings & Bailey. With leather tabs labeled "soups," "meats," "fish," etc., the publisher modestly advertised that the blank book was "the only scientific and perfect form of book for preservation of recipes ever made." Roberts filled its pages with recipes and household hints collected from Good Housekeeping, some from "Auntie" and "Mama," and these two complimentary recipes from that vacation meal.

Although I'm not positive who Mabel Roberts was, my "prime suspect" is Mabel Junkins, who was born in 1881 to Baltimore pickle manufacturer J. Wm. Junkins and his wife Alice V. Davis. Mabel married William Calvert Roberts and lived in the Roland Park neighborhood of Baltimore. She passed away in 1959. J. William Junkins was originally from Biddeford Maine, which is less than 100 miles from the White Mountains of New Hampshire.

When the Mount Washington Hotel was being built in the White Mountains, the Brooklyn Daily Eagle declared it a "modern palatial house" to rival the tourist palaces found at Niagara and Yosemite. "From the dining room… one looks into Jefferson Notch and across the green golf links to the Presidential range." In addition to the dining and ballrooms, the hotel boasted offices and "public rooms," 350 sleeping rooms with "the modern requirement of private baths."

The hotel opened in 1902, built in nearly the same spot where Ethan Allen Crawford had operated an inn in the mid-1800s. The Crawford family had moved to the area as pioneers working the trade route, but eventually, they became a crucial part of developing the White Mountains into a New England tourist destination where people could escape the stresses of bustling cities like Baltimore.

According to Dona Brown in "Inventing New England," in the nineteenth century, "an entirely new kind of tourism was shaping the region. This new tourism was driven by a profound 'sentimentalization' of… a mythic region called Old New England – rural, preindustrial, and ethnically 'pure' – a reverse image of all that was most unsettling in late nineteenth-century urban life."

At first a destination for mountain-climbers, the White Mountains became a place that remained geographically wild but "overflowing with noisy, unquiet company… and… all kinds of noisy pleasures." "Champagne corks fly about at the hotels, gentlemen sit and play cards in the middle of the day, ladies talk about dress-makers and fashions," according to Frederika Bremer in 1849.

In the 1910s, travelers could spend time playing tennis or golf, hiking or taking a rail trip to Mount Washington's summit. At the hotel, amenities included a ballroom, indoor pool, and meals prepared by a European chef who the New York Tribune declared had "the prestige of a chef from Delmonico's." In fact, the closest recipe I could find to this remoulade formula is in Delmonico's chef Charles Ranhofer's 1894 tome "The Epicurean."

Mabel Roberts may have reached the hotel by taking the famous B&O Royal Blue line to New York and transferring to the Connecticut River Line, or she could have followed the Evening Sun's 1919 advice to take a boat to Boston and complete the journey on the Maine Central Railway. The trip by train or boat would have been accompanied by fashionable meals, time spent in library-smoker-observation or parlor cars, and socializing with other travelers.

But there was another option. In 1906, the Tribune wrote that "more than forty automobiles of regular guests in the Bretton Woods garage tell the store of motoring the hills and the hold it has upon the summer visitors here." Brochures and newspaper guides provided maps of scenic routes for "tours" en route to and from the many vacation destinations. In 1917, a Baltimore Sun headline declared: "Vacation In Car Ideal." "Expense of Month Costs Price of Railroad Fares," read the subtitle. The next year, a similar article noted that "practically everything possible has been done by state and town officials to add to the comfort of automobile tourists." The Sun "Hotel and Resort Bureau" offered travel assistance to readers by phone.

The rise of the auto age may have brought clientele to the grand old hotels, but cars also helped usher in their decline. Dona Brown wrote that "instead of large numbers of stationary guests who stayed for a month or more, the automobile brought unpredictable, vagrant overnight guests." While the "old-fashioned Victorian hotels had been designed with public interaction with strangers in mind," cars "made it possible to frame the entire touring experience, even getting there, in complete privacy... automobiles fostered industries that provided greater privacy on arrival" like motels, cottages and boarding houses.

"Most of the great White Mountain hotels burned down. Such large frame structures had always been susceptible to winter fires (often suspiciously well-timed to wipe out financial obligations without much danger to guests or workers), but by the end of the nineteenth century they were no longer being rebuilt," wrote Brown.

One of the rare survivors is, in fact, the Mount Washington Hotel, which still stands in all its splendor on a mountain that Nathanial Hawthorne declared an "undecaying monument" to its namesake. ✿

Fried Sea Bass:

"Split fish and remove bones – Dip in flour then in egg then in bread crumbs."

Remoulade:

"Blanche one shallot – anchovy paste to give flavor & color – 2 yolks of hard boiled eggs _ = raw eggs
Pinch English mustard salt and pepper to taste blended with tarragon vinegar – consistency of mayonnaise dressing add parsley chives"

Recipes from "Mabel Roberts Cookbook," n.d., Maryland Historical Society MS 2755

Mount Washington Hotel Postcard c. 1920s

Grape Fruit Candy, Harriet Caperton Shaw

Posted on Oct 18, 2017

A run-in with a bad head-cold scared me back into eating massive quantities of citrus fruit. After carefully removing the flesh and juice from a half-dozen grapefruits I figured I would finally try a common old recipe: candied citrus peel. Lemon and orange had been popular options in all of my oldest cookbooks but in the early 20th-century grapefruit really began to catch on.

Baltimore at that time had more diverse produce options than you would expect. While citrus fruit from Florida was a huge industry, the ports at the Inner Harbor were just as likely to receive shipments from Jamaica along with other items like coconuts and bananas. Occasionally fruit was even smuggled in. Many failed fruit smuggling efforts were reported in the pages of the Baltimore Sun from the late 1800s through 1910s.

In September of 1909 the Baltimore Sun reported that "Grape fruit is more popular each season, and is no longer considered a luxury, as formerly."

For the most part, as you would expect, grapefruit was eaten for breakfast, juiced, or served more pretentiously scooped out and combined with other fruits back in their halved rind. If using both the fruit and the peel was not sufficient, the women's page of the Sun had the following DIY hint in 1913: "the seeds of grapefruit have an æsthetic use which the lowly apple core has not, for if planted they will grow into a beautiful green vine."

By 1931 the local grocery store Hopper & McGaw listed grapefruit as a "Thanksgiving specialty," along with raisins, mince meat, figs and nuts.

The cookbook I got my candied peel recipe from is not dated, but the call number at the Pratt Library implies it is from 1920. Entitled "The Tried and True Recipe Book," it was compiled by the Woman's Guild of the Church of St. Michael and All Angels in Baltimore. Lots of the surnames ring familiar to me from street names, Maryland families, and other recipes in my collection:

Mosher, Sothoron, Diffenderffer, etc.

This recipe (as well as many others in the book ranging from soups to sweets) was contributed by Mrs. J. J. Forbes Shaw, the wife of a Baltimore banker and tobacco merchant. Born Harriet Alexander Hereford in Union WV in 1874, she hailed from well-known families. Her father, Frank Hereford was a senator and congressman. Her grandfather on her mother's side, Hugh Elmwood Caperton, was also a congressman. The maternal side of her family are ancestors of William Gaston Caperton III, the governor of West Virginia from 1989-1997.

Harriet married James John Forbes Shaw in 1907, and the family lived at 1809 N. Calvert Street. They were fairly prominent, turning up in society columns in the Sun. In 1921, however, their mentions took a turn for the tragic.

Their 12-year old daughter Alice Caperton Shaw drowned when a rowboat containing the girl, her two sisters and three other children capsized on the Servern River. Reverend Wyatt Brown, whose photo appears in the front of "The Tried and True Recipe Book," rescued the other five children. The many newspapers that covered the incident reported that he was a nervous wreck after the incident, covered in scratches from the children's grasps.

Twelve years after the harrowing incident, in April 1933, Harriet Shaw died at age 59. Mr. Shaw did not recover from the pain of these deaths. On September 20th, 1937, he visited the graves of his wife and daughter at Greenmount Cemetery. Eventually, he kneeled on the ground, pulled out a pistol and shot himself in the head. The cemetery superintendent who had been watching Shaw pace in the cemetery cried out, but it was too late. Shaw left a note pinned to his clothing, stating simply "The act is my own."

The Shaw home on 1809 N. Calvert Street is no longer standing, but nearby, The Church of St. Michael & All Angels is still there at 2013 St. Paul. The reverend who saved the surviving daughters from the 1921 boat accident is most likely Hunter Wyatt-Brown. He was known for weaving the "Lost Cause" ideology into his sermons, and Mrs. Shaw had been a member of Daughters of the Confederacy. Today, The Church of St. Michael & All Angels serves a multicultural congregation.

Although Wyatt-Brown left Maryland to become a bishop in Harrisburg Pennsylvania, his son Bertram Wyatt-Brown returned to Baltimore to study history at Johns Hopkins. In "The Society for U.S. Intellectual History" in 2015, Andrew Hartman wrote of Bertram Wyatt-Brown's work: "Bert... zeroed in on the tragic and gothic South, as well as a host of men and women, gnarled by death, humiliation, loss, and anxieties. His books are populated by the chronically depressed, and by tortured writers on the brink of suicide, or novelists who were as much at war with the self as the region they called home." ✸

Grape Fruit Candy

After taking out the meat of the grape fruit cut rind in long pieces. Cover it with a strong salt water and let it soak 12 hours. Change water every 12 hours until rinds have soaked in strong brine 48 hours. Take rinds out of salt water and cover with fresh cold water and let it boil 10 minutes. Change water and let it boil another 10 minutes. Do this 6 times. Then take it out and weigh rinds and put a pound of sugar to every pound of fruit. Let cook slowly until the syrup, formed by putting sugar on rinds, has boiled away. Then take out piece by piece of grape fruit and roll in granulated sugar.

Recipe from "The Tried and True Recipe Book," Woman's Guild, Church of St. Michael and All Angels, Baltimore

---

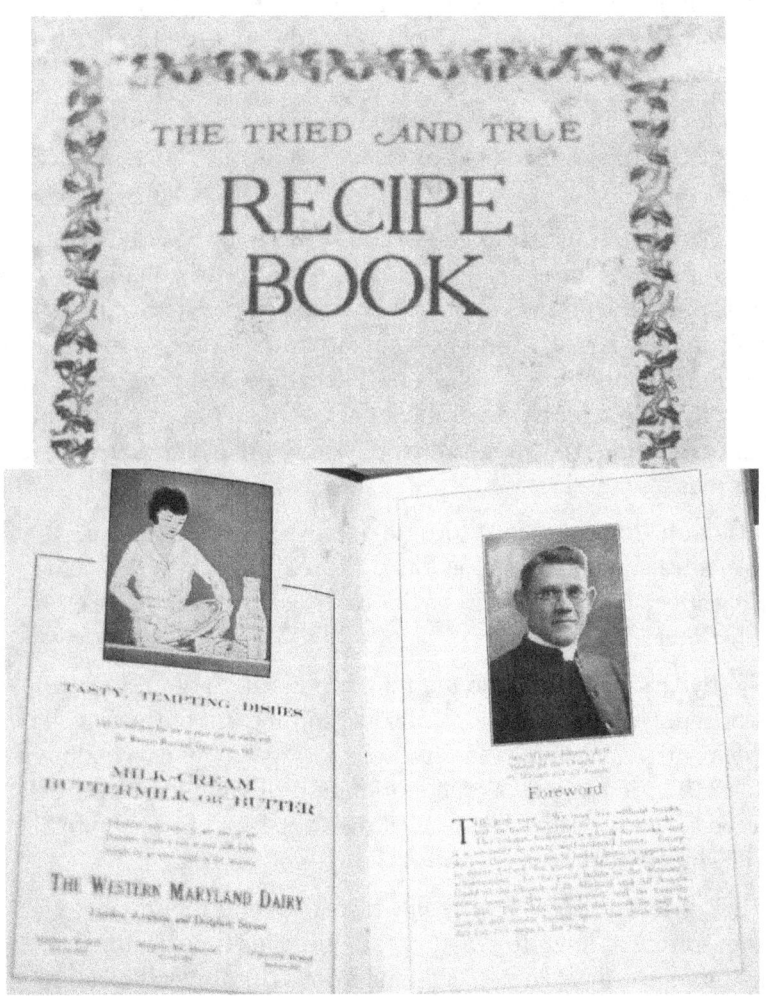

Cindy Knopp's White Sweet Potato Coconut Pie

Posted on November 23, 2022

For 36 years, columnist and photographer Brice Stump wrote about life on the Eastern Shore. In his columns, he explored its history – including the Civil War, and pondered the petty tribulations of modern life.

On one topic in particular, Stump was passionate: White Hayman Sweet Potatoes. Having been raised on a farm, Stump admitted they aren't easy to grow. But of their flavor, he sang the praises.

"Unlike the familiar orange-fleshed sweet potatoes that required marshmallows, brown sugar and lots of butter to enhance their nutty flavor, the Hayman tickles the palate with a natural, delicately sweet taste and heavenly texture," Stump wrote in the Salisbury Daily Times in 1999. In that article, he interviewed Rev. Sally Bowen, a descendent of Daniel Hayman, the ship captain purported to have brought the potatoes from North Carolina to Maryland in the 1850s.

Although stories trace White Haymans to North Carolina, nary a trace of them can be found there now. White Haymans are a specialty of the Eastern Shore, "raised only for Shore consumers," wrote Stump.

Eight years later he bemoaned the proliferation of O'Henrys appearing on the market, ironically "coming out of the Carolinas, apparently." These pretenders were giving Haymans a bad name. An authenticity test was recommended: "If you put pressure down on your thumb and draw it over the face of a Hayman, it will 'skin' easily, whereas the O'Henry wont."

If the difference is so stark, that casts a lot of doubt on my last attempt at a white sweet potato pie. This time around, my mom acquired some Haymans from Whiteraven's Nest in Chincoteague, Virginia – along with several other varieties of sweet potato. So I used a blend. She was warned to cure them several weeks, in a warm and dry place, or else risk defeating the point of even tasting them.

The 1921 book "The Sweet Potato: A Handbook for the Practical Grower" by T.E. Hand and K.L. Cockerham agreed. The book stated that Haymans were also being marketed as "Southern Queen" and advised "it is much improved in eating quality by storage and though not a very choice eating potato in fall and early winter, it becomes very good indeed in late winter and spring."

Bernard Herman's 2020 book "A South You Never Ate" has a chapter dedicated to Haymans. Herman's neighbors also lamented that sellers were passing off O'Henrys as the hard-to-get Hayman. William Harmon, one of the last farmers growing the coveted item, told Herman of the finicky nature of the plant itself. "Now Hayman potato, he won't grow fast. He take his time," Harmon said.

At one point in time, a large portion of Virginia's Eastern Shore economy depended on potatoes (sweet and not) grown for New York Markets. The 1884 railroad had made transport northward swift and reliable. In 1928, fourteen thousand boxcars left the peninsula carrying Irish potatoes. The labor was largely done by Black field hands, tenant farmers or owners of small farms.

Herman's book delves deeper into the growing, curing and cooking of Haymans. It is a great read.

Thanks to Herman's book, I broke one of my cardinal rules of cookbook acquisition and I purchased a non-Maryland cookbook. My copy of Fairy Mapp White's 1958 "Foolproof Cookbook" is a gem though, signed by the author, with a few handwritten corrections within. Faded cover and discolored spine, it smells like the Nancy Drew books I used to read as a girl. Anyhow, it was printed in Baltimore.

White included instructions for baking sweet potatoes, "Hamans and Spanish": "Potatoes should be put into a hot oven dripping wet, heat reduced some in about 15 or 20 minutes. I learned from a substitute maid Christmas 1953 that greasing Spanish and Haman potatoes with left-over sausage or bacon drippings made them bake and peel better."

White noted that "as far as [she knows] Haman and Spanish potatoes are raised only on the Eastern Shore of Virginia." She also remarked that the potatoes "are hard to find now" – now being 1958, when her book was published.

I made this pie before I had a copy of "Foolproof Cookbook." Recipes particular to white sweet potatoes are hard to come by – or too easy, if you take into account that for many Eastern Shore residents, the requirement doesn't even need to be mentioned.

Still, I decided to try a recipe from Cindy Knopp, a farmer who was interviewed by the Baltimore Sun in 1988. Cindy and her husband Robert Knopp, Jr. grew several varieties of sweet potatoes and sold them at the downtown farmers' market that year. Like many articles mentioning the Hayman, that one suggested they be baked – not boiled.

In 2015, after the Salisbury Daily Times was acquired by "media holding company" Gannett, Brice Harpers job was basically eliminated to make way for the "Newsroom of the Future." Rhapsodizing about sweet potatoes just doesn't drive clicks (I should know).

While the digital era has taken away some things, it gives others. Within minutes I am able to pull up many of Harper's various articles mentioning Haymans. They join the canon of Hayman lore, right along with Fairy Mapp White's own recollection "Home from public school, known as Grange Hall, on the old Keller Fair Grounds, nothing was more satisfying for a snack than a home made sausage and a juicy Haman." Like the Hayman, folksy storytelling may not produce profits for the shareholders, but it lives on. ❈

White Sweet Potato Coconut Pie

3 cups cooked, mashed white sweet potatoes (about 1.5 lbs)
1 cup flaked coconut
1 teaspoon coconut extract
1/2 teaspoon nutmeg
1/2 teaspoon ginger
3/4 cup milk
3/4 cup white sugar
1 large egg
2 tablespoons margarine
1 9-inch unbaked deep dish pie shell
Heat oven to 350°.
Mash sweet potato flesh – for a smoother pie, strain through a sieve.
Add all other ingredients and beat on high speed until mixed.
Pour mixture into pie shell and bake for 50 to 55 minutes. Serve topped with whipped cream and additional coconut.

Recipe Adapted from the Baltimore Sun, 1988

Lillian Lottier's Tropicaroma Cake

Posted on February 16, 2016

Before the internet and magazines boasted millions of novel (and disposable) recipes, newspapers were a valuable source for recipes that could become staples in a household.

This one was shared in 1939 in the Afro-American by Lillian Lottier, prominent Baltimorean, teacher, activist, and columnist for that paper.

Lottier's "Royal Tropicaroma Cake" was first popularized in "The Royal [Baking Powder] Guide to Meal Planning" in 1929 as "Tropic Aroma" cake. I expected pineapples & bananas but this is actually more of a spice cake complimented with coffee and chocolate.

Lillian, born in 1881, was the daughter of Reverend Reuben Armstrong, who came to Baltimore from Harrisburg, PA to become pastor of historically black Madison Avenue Presbyterian Church from 1897 to 1904. According to the church's website, the ministry of Armstrong was "riveted in the policies of black middle classness and intellectualism. [He] encouraged and sponsored ecumenical involvement, wholesome cooperation, and cultural activities – including forums and literary and musical programs."

It was from this tradition that Lillian Lottier dedicated herself to a life of working for civil rights and social progress. In 1924, Lottier served as the first female president of the Baltimore NAACP. There she "led the Branch for only a single term but made a tremendous statement and mark on the Branch and the City of Baltimore." She was a founding member of the Baltimore Urban League, and remained active with that organization as well as the Women's Presbyterian Society.

"Her social activism gives an insight into the interest of female members of the NAACP. She was a long-time member of the United Protestant group in Baltimore that raised funds for inter-church meetings and charity work starting in 1933 and was executive

officer by World War II. During the great depression Lottier was a member of National Negro Congress and was a publicity officer for its Baltimore branch, spearheading campaigns to end racial discrimination in employment, targeting large corporations such as Consolidated Gas, Electric Light, and Power Company [now BGE]."
– Borders of Equality: The NAACP and the Baltimore Civil Rights Struggle, 1914-1970

Outside of her own column, Lillian Lottier merited frequent mentions in the Afro-American due to her active involvement in the PTA of several Baltimore schools. Her namesake daughter, Lillian Lottier Bolden (1918-2000) was an educator herself, who taught physically and mentally challenged students in Baltimore City.

"Teachers participated in a wide range of efforts to promote democracy, reform curricula, organize communities, and mentor young civil rights activists. Their engagement, both in the public sphere and behind the scenes, has shaped and influenced the Civil Rights Movement." – Teachers in the Movement: A civil rights oral history project

Reading through Lottier's columns in the Afro-American is a reminder of the diverse viewpoints among those working for civil rights. "Borders of Equality" described some of her activism with contraception as being "in the vein of the middle-class progressive urge of the era," and some of Lottier's views might not seem progressive to those with a modern view of civil rights causes.

Nonetheless, her column is an interesting insight into the generation that laid the groundwork for the civil rights activism of the 1960s. In one spirited column she decries a preacher making a flirtatious "remark" to a parishioner. She passionately censures this affront to morality. Despite the amount of words dedicated to this outrage, the "remark" seems to be lost to time. I for one feel cheated.

"Now, she's a person that puzzles me. I have often wondered whether she is a saint or a sinner. There are times when she seems pious enough to be a cardinal, and there are times when she seems to have a devil-may-care glint in her eye and a 'Come-on, I-dare' look in her face." – 1930 Afro-American column about Lillian Lottier.

Lillian was married to George V. Lottier, a postal worker. Although he was involved with the YMCA and a writers group called the "Scribblers," he does not appear to have been as outspoken as his wife. The family lived at 1509 Druid Hill Avenue in the Upton neighborhood.

"Even though this sex of ours has convincingly demonstrated our ability to compete successfully with men in almost every phase of life, there are still a few dull-witted, pig-headed, narrow-minded males left for whom we welcome additional proof." – Lillian Lottier, 1926

The frequent Afro-American coverage of Lillian Lottier's active life began to taper off in the 1950s. An avid-reader, she remained active in book clubs and celebrated milestones in the lives of her four children. In 1957, the Lottiers' 50th anniversary was celebrated in the paper. Lillian passed away in 1976 with little fanfare. A Baltimore Sun obituary stated that in addition to her four children, she was survived by twelve-grandchildren and fifteen great-grandchildren.

"At the best our gain in knowledge during a short life-time is but partial and limited, and it does seem a shame to waste any precious hours in willful blindness and self-deception.

Let it be our earnest desire... to do our feebly best to live fully, deeply, richly, and in accordance with the Creator's wonderful purpose for mankind." – Lillian Lottier, 1926 ✤

Afro-American, 1957

Worthwhile beliefs, standards kept Lottiers together 50 years

BALTIMORE

"Have worthwhile beliefs and standards and practice them faithfully day by day.

"Be always ready for wholesome advice."

This is the advice of Mrs. Lillian Lottier who with her husband, George Sr. 2433 Calverton Heights Ave. celebrated their 50th wedding anniversary November 20.

Some 19 members of the family gathered for the celebration here in Baltimore at the home of their son and daughter - in - law, Mr. and Mrs. George Lottier Jr., 2422 Harlem Ave. Wednesday.

AS SHE prepared for the family dinner in her honor, Mrs. Lottier laughingly said: "Just think, after 50 years, I don't have to cook a meal."

Of her other celebration plans, Mrs. Lottier said: "For the next week, we are going to take a 50th wedding trip to NYC and see all of our relatives there," she stated. The Lottiers left on Friday, and Mrs. Lottier had bubbled over as she described the forthcoming trip.

She stated that they will visit Dr. George Haynes, in Vernon, N.Y.; a sister, Florence Petersen in NYC have Thanksgiving d with another sister and b er - in - law. Mrs. W er J. Blondin also in N

"My husband had wante take the trip last winter. we decided to wait spring. We didn't g chance to go then and t it over and decided we s make it en our 50th ann sary," Mrs. Lottier states "We are happy and tha that we are well and abl go," she continued.

MR. LOTTIER retired years ago after serving al 50 years in the Post Offi

Asked about his activi Mrs. Lottier exclaimed, "h most lives at the Mary Baptist Home for Aged Pe where he is secretary, Mason, Pythian and activ Leadenhall Baptist Churc

Mrs. Lottier was form assistant director in the partment of Christian S Relations at the Council Churches, is presently on board of the Barrett Scho Girls.

She is also a membe Grace Presbyterian Chur Mrs. Lottier explained since her father, the Rev. ben H. Armstrong was a byterian minister, she mained in that church an husband was a Baptist. The Rev. Mr. Armstrong

Tropicaroma Cake

.75 Cup butter
1.25 Cup sugar
2 egg
2.5 Cup flour
4 Teaspoon baking powder
.25 Teaspoon salt
1 Teaspoon nutmeg
1 Teaspoon cinnamon
1 Cup milk
1 Tablespoon cocoa
1 Tablespoon boiling water

For icing:
2 Tablespoon butter
2 Cup sugar, powdered
1 Tablespoon cocoa
1 Tablespoon vanilla extract
1 Tablespoon strong coffee

Cream butter; add sugar a little at a time followed by well beaten eggs, mixing thoroughly.

Sift flour, salt, baking powder and spices together. Add a little of the dry ingredients to the first mixture; slowly add milk followed by remaining dry ingredients.

Pour two-thirds of this batter into two greased and floured layer tins. To remaining third of batter, add 1 tablespoon cocoa mixed with 1 tablespoon of boiling water. Use this batter for middle layer.

Bake layers at 375 F for 15-20 minutes. Put the filling and icing between layers and on top and sides of the cake.

Filling/Icing: Cream butter and add sugar and cocoa very slowly, beating until light and fluffy. Slowly add vanilla and coffee until soft enough to spread.

Recipe adapted from "Cake for a Postman," Baltimore Afro-American newspaper, 1939

Risotto, "Collge Cookery"

Posted on June 15, 2018

"Boxes of confectionery, cake, etc., sent to students, so far from being the kindness intended, are a positive source of evil. Their contents, eaten, as is generally the case, irregularly and late at night, produce sickness and impair scholarship, perhaps more than any other single cause. Unless parents and friends heed this remark, we shall be obliged to make the reception of such boxes and parcels by the pupils ground for animadversion." – Connecticut Literary Institution 1870-71 catalog, quoted in "College Girls" by Lynn Peril

After several failed attempts to found a women's college in Baltimore, the Baltimore Conference of the Methodist Episcopal Church finally succeeded in 1885. The main building on St. Paul Street was constructed to harmonize architecturally with the First Church (now Lovely Lane Methodist.)

According to the 1905 book "The College Girl In America And The Institutions Which Make Her What She Is," the school's co-founder Dr. John F. Goucher did not hold many other women's' colleges in high regard. His philosophy was paraphrased: "The ordinary girls' college turns out... an occasional scholar, some pedants, many teachers, and a few – a very few – all-around girls... Every effort is made at this college to develop appreciation, ripe culture, and womanliness."

Nonetheless, sources indicate that life at the "Women's College of Baltimore City" was not too different than at other women's colleges. "The History of Goucher College" by Anna Knipp and Thaddeus P. Thomas describes rigorous academics. At 659 pages, Knipp and Thomas' 1939 history book IS rigorous academics. One aspect that I grasped before dozing off was that the school had a special focus on physical fitness.

Considerations for student health at women's colleges was not entirely out of the ordinary. Wellesley College founder Henry Durant believed that health was critical to learning, stating that "pies, lies, and doughnuts should never have a place at Wellesley

College."

Out of context, this sounds a like a bizarre fixation, but in fact, snacking and junk food had been the secret scourge of women's colleges from the beginning. Some schools implemented rules that barred families from sending foods. This only resulted in clandestine dormitory makeshift meals known as "spreads."

Often made in a chafing dish, with tools on hand (think nail files and powder boxes), the late-night meals became a central part of social life in women's colleges at the beginning of the 20th century. In a 1906 article in Ladies Home Journal, called "Christmas Pranks of College Girls," one student reported that "spreads were forbidden and the halls were vigorously patrolled for the suppression of them."

Fudge is by far the most famous and enduring result of dormitory snacking, and a popular origin story credits the candy to Vassar students.

Fudge was not the only food served up – it wasn't even the only candy. In "College Cookery," a 1912 cookbook printed in Baltimore, there are six recipes for chocolate fudge, as well as recipes for taffy, toasted marshmallows, sandwiches, Welsh Rarebit (a popular chafing dish item), as well as several recipes "brought from Italy by a member of Goucher College." Of these recipes from Italy, I opted to try the risotto.

"College Cookery" was compiled by Harriet A. Blogg from Norfolk VA. Blogg's date of birth varies wildly across censuses, but her family moved to Baltimore in the late 1800s. Her father Edward N. S. Blogg was a preacher from Germany and her mother Charlotte Collins Thayer hailed from the large Massachusetts family of Colonel Collins Thayer. The family became prominent in Baltimore. From their home base on 2506 St. Paul Street, the Bloggs engaged and entertained doctors and Peabody Professors, women's college clubs and charitable organizations. Harriet's brother Percy T. Blogg was a "sportsman, naturalist, essayist, and poet" according to his 1947 Baltimore Sun obituary. Another brother, Edward R. F. Blogg, was a bookseller whose frequent business travels and illnesses were regularly reported in the Baltimore Sun society pages.

Harriet and her sister Minnie were both librarians. Minnie was one of the first librarians for the Johns Hopkins Hospital Library which became the Welch Medical Library in 1929. She worked with doctors to compile bibliographies for their publications. After she retired in 1935, she volunteered at the Johns Hopkins Nurses Home Library until shortly before her death in 1959.

As for Harriet, she was a librarian for Goucher from 1896-1917, and a correspondent for the Baltimore Sun. She too was involved with medical research work. At Goucher, she founded the Press Club in 1898. According to her 1935 obituary, she was "well known in literary circles."

As the publication of a cookbook glorifying College Cookery might tip you off, late night dormitory snack-parties eventually became an accepted, even sanctioned, part of college life.
As Lynn Peril wrote in "College Girls": "The 1947 edition of Stephens College's Within the Ivy student handbook called the spread 'one of the joys of college life' proving without a doubt that its authority-flouting nature was deader than a doorknob."

Needless to say, this coincided with the slow demise of the tradition. Next Friday, when I'm watching all the co-eds at the liquor store conceal their purchases deep inside backpacks, part of me will wish that their rule-flouting could ever be so beneficial to humanity, to popularize something like fudge. ✻

Risotto (Italian Rice)

(Brought from Italy by member of Goucher College)

1/2 cup rice
1 onion
2 tablespoonfuls Grated Cheese (Parmesan)
1 qt. Beef stock—(may be beef extract)
Zaferano, pinch (may be purchased at Itl. shop)*
Chop onion and brown in butter. Add rice dry (don't wash it), and cook until brown. Add beef stock and boil until soft. Add part of cheese and the powder. Serve with remainder of cheese on top. This is delicious.

Recipe from "College Cookery", 1912, compiled by H.A.B.

*I had to look this up. It's saffron!

Crabs & Bacon, Miss H.A. Blogg

Posted on June 28, 2021

There has probably been no greater force for the dissemination of recipes developed by home cooks than recipe contests.

State and county fairs in the 19th century hosted many cooking contests as a part of their "ladies" programming. These fairs were an opportunity for women gather and to show off their "domestic arts", from needlework to baking and cooking. In my research about White Potato Pie, I came across a "white potato custard pie" category at the 1880 Cecil County Agricultural Society exhibition. The level of specificity suggests a large amount of prizes to be awarded. The other pie categories that year were Green Peach, Dried Peach, Green Apple, Dried Apple, Grape, Cherry, Gooseberry, Currant, Pumpkin, Cocoanut, Lemon, and Apple – and that is just for pies. There were contests for preserves, cakes, breads, cheeses, and more. The dollar prize adjusts to about twenty dollars in "today money." Considering the amount of effort to just travel to these events, it was clear that the glory of winning was an incentive as well.

It wasn't long before companies selling ingredients and kitchen appliances figured out that they could use contests as a way to get publicity – and to crowdsource recipes to promote their products. Companies like Heinz, Borden, and Kraft have held recipe contests over the decades. Sometimes, the winning recipes ended up published in promotional cookbooks and advertisements. Newspapers used recipe contests as a way to engage women readers. Home economists and cooking teachers were often employed as judges.

In November 1910, hundreds of women showed up to the Bernheimer Brothers store in downtown Baltimore to enter their bread loaves, biscuits, pies, doughnuts, and cakes to be judged by "representatives of local newspapers." The Baltimore Sun described some of the cakes as "ornamental in the extreme" and touted the "skill shown by Baltimore women" but did not print the names of any of the winners or the names of the winning items.

Perhaps the Sun was inspired by the success of this contest to hold their own contest in early 1911.

Newspapers had been having similar contests since the 1890s. In 1901, the San Francisco Examiner used a format similar to the one the Sun would later use: a series of weekly contests in different categories, the recipes delivered to the paper by mail. The winning recipes – including addresses and names of the winners, were printed in a lavishly illustrated spread in the Sunday women's pages. The Examiner advertised their contest series as "the biggest thing ever heard of." What newspaper could resist trying to replicate "the biggest thing ever heard of?"

The Sun asked its 1911 readers "Are You A Good Cook?" and offered a $5 prize for the winner, with five one-dollar runner-up awards. The twenty-three weekly contests were judged by Miss Lillian Armstrong, director of the Y.W.C.A. School of Domestic Science. It is unknown whether the recipes were judged by actually tasting them. Around fifty recipes were printed each week, so it doesn't seem likely that Miss Armstrong and company had time to test the entries. Perhaps she used her domestic expertise to envision the recipe results.

Over the contest's 23-week run, there were 1541 recipes printed. I've come across these newspaper pages many times, while researching other recipes. After noticing that a lot of the addresses were around my neighborhood, Charles Village, I decided I wanted to see the contest recipes on a map. The resulting map shows just under six hundred of the recipe winners around Baltimore. Other entries came from all over the state, with a few from other places as far away as Wisconsin. The Frederick (Maryland) Post often listed the names of women from Frederick who'd won that week's contest.

When researching some of the participants in the recipe contest, I found a few "prominent citizens," as well as some people who appeared to be domestic servants or first-generation German immigrants. The early 1900s were a pivotal time in the development of Baltimore city's segregationist politics, and as scholars have pointed out, the Sun played a role. Like the newspaper's readership at the time, contest participants were most likely to be white.

Thanks to a generous friend, I had a lot of crab-meat and decided to try one of the crab recipes. I made "Crabs And Bacon," a recipe contributed by Miss H. A. Blogg of 2506 St. Paul Street.

When I went to research Miss (Harriet) A. Blogg, I was led to... my own blog post, "Risotto," from "College Cookery." Miss Blogg was a librarian at Goucher College who clearly had an interest in food. In addition to entering this contest, and compiling the "College Cookery" cookbook, she wrote for magazines and newspapers, often about the dining trends of college girls. I'll try not to worry too much about how I managed to forget a name like that, and instead I will continue to marvel that out of fifteen-hundred-plus recipes, I managed to pick one by someone I'd already written about.

After sharing my map with Charles Village neighbors, I've already heard from a few people who found a recipe from their address. I hope to hear from more. I would love to bring some recipes from 110 years ago forward through time, right to their home kitchens. ❖

Crabs & Bacon

1 Quart crab meat
2 Tablespoon butter
salt
pepper, white
.5 Lb bacon
parsley

Take 1 quart crab meat, having it in large white flakes, and put it in a porcelain saucepan with 2 tablespoonfuls of butter. Season with salt and white pepper to taste and let it simmer for 10 minutes. Take 1/2 pound of very thinly sliced bacon and fry quickly in a hot pan. Pile the crab meat in the centre of a round platter, arrange the bacon in a border around it and put several long sprays of parsley attractively on the crab. This is an original dish and as delicious as it is beautiful.

Recipe from the Baltimore Sun 1911 Recipe Contest Series, May 28th. Second prize winner, submitted by Harriet A. Blogg.

PRIZE WINNERS IN CRAB RECIPE CONTEST

FIRST PRIZE—$5

SECOND PRIZE—$1
Crabs and Bacon.

MISS H. A. BLOGG,
2208 St. Paul street.

THIRD PRIZE—$1
Crab Salad.

MISS AGNES N. POSEY,
Laurel, Md.

FOURTH PRIZE—$1

MRS. M. E. NOSCHER,
644 Fulton street.

Maryland Filled Fried Hard Crabs.

MRS. J. T. STOCKETT,
Maryland avenue.

Baked Crabs.

MRS. J. D. N. STRAYHAM,
Spring Hill, Charles county, Md.

Southern Maryland Crab Croquettes.

MRS. JULIA HILLS,
Spring Hill, Md.

Crabs with Peas.

MRS. C. V. DOYLE,
Brooklyn, N. Y.

Maryland Crab-Meat Croquettes.

MRS. J. H. BENNETT,
Roseville, Md.

Maryland Style Crab Cakes.

MRS. E. WALTER,
1011 West Fairmount avenue.

To Cook Hard Crabs.

MRS. E. WALTER,
1011 West Fairmount avenue.

Deviled Crabs.

MISS M. WILLSON,
113 Dark Carey street.

Baked Soft Crabs.

MRS. WILLIAM A. LEMMON,
430 Calhoun street.

Crab Cakes.

MRS. M. E. TAVENDER,
2009 North Charles street.

Deviled Crabs.

MRS. MARIE NAWROWEZCK,
2039 Westwood avenue.

Crab Pie.

CHARLOTTE H. FRIEND,
2021 Guilford avenue.

Crab Fritters.

MRS. B. W. WOODWARD,
570 South Irvin ave. Baltimore, Md.

Crabs au Gratin.

MRS. C. V. DOYLE.

Devilled Way of Serving Crabs.

MRS. WILLIAM STONEY,
Corbettsville, Md.

Baltimore Crab Rissoles.

MISS MARTHA E. HOPKINS,
245 South Ann street.

A Delicious Way of Serving Crabs.

F. T. COOPER,
1017 West Fayette street.

Crab Flakes a la Newburg, Hot Chafing Dish.

MRS. E. T. THOMPSON,
7994 West Lexington street.

Fried Crabs.

W. NEILSON,
1817 North Calvert street.

Soft-Shell Crabs, Fried.

EDITH V. SWITZER,
Walbrook.

Crab Salad.

MRS. W. H. CROX,
1010 West Fayette street.

Crabs in a Francaise.

MRS. E. M. SUMNER,
Emory Md.

Pickled Crabs.

MRS. WALKER,
1309 North Ensor street.

Crab Meat en Casserole.

F. E. BARNES,
2036 North Fulton avenue.

Crab Omelet.

KATHARINE M. LEE.

Maryland Crab Cakes.

MRS. J. J. MITCHELL,
2730 Huntingdon avenue.

Deviled Crabs.

SALLIE E. KNEASE,
128 Whatley street, New Haven, Conn.

Crab Salad.

MRS. J. R. BISHOP,
Sherwood, Md.

Prize-Winning Recipes Were Selected By Miss I. Clair Sansbury, Graduate Of The Samuel Ready School, And Instructor In Domestic Science In The Baltimore Schools.

Are You A Good Cook?

THE prize winners in the Sunday Sun's contest for crabs are given today. The Sun now wants the best recipe for sweet pickles.

Five dollars will be paid for the secret. The woman sending the five next best sweet pickle recipes will be paid $1 each.

Remember—
$5.00 for the best pickle recipe.
$1.00 for each of the five next best.

If you do not get an award on this week's contest, try again.

Recipe for sweet pickles must be in The Sun office by June 5. Address Prize Recipe Editor, The Sunday Sun.

One Hundred Dollar Fudge

Posted on November 13, 2016

In 1971, a woman in Fruitland, MD, recovering from an illness, took out an ad in the Salisbury Daily Times to express gratitude towards the "many friends who contributed in any way" towards her recovery. She thanked friends, neighbors, ambulance drivers, doctors, her Pastor, and she praised the Lord. She also thanked "Bill Phillips and the many Party Line listeners" – for the cards, flowers, phone calls and cash donations that they provided in her time of need.

For over thirty years, Party Line was one of the most popular radio shows on the Eastern Shore. Hosted by onetime station manager William Phillips on the WICO country music station, "Party Line" served as a forum where listeners could call in to buy, sell and swap anything from outboard motors to exotic birds. The idea of Craigslist as a morning talk show may seem confusing, but by all accounts, the show's popularity could be attributed to Phillips himself, who charmed listeners with "folksy chit-chat" – and a sense of community so strong that it mobilized listeners to care for one-another in times of need. An oft-repeated anecdote about the show involves a woman who called to report that her husband lost his dentures on the beach – later found by another Party Line listener, of course.

The nature of radio broadcasts is somewhat ephemeral – and an on-air flea-market even more so. But the show has left behind a lasting legacy in the form of a beloved cookbook sourced from its many listeners. Eastern Shore natives still seek out copies and share memories of the tattered copies of this book serving faithfully in their family kitchens. According to the book's preface, "What is Cooking On Party Line" received 1400 contributions from listeners.

The resulting book gives an overview of what was cooking in Eastern Shore kitchens around 1983. From the first recipe for "Cheddar Cheese Balls" to the final recipe, "Red Pepper Jelly," the collection demonstrates that food habits from a particular time and place can't be easily pigeonholed or stereotyped. While there are many convenience recipes associated with the 1970s, featuring processed ingredients such as Kool-Aid and Cheez-Whiz, there are also recipes that have obviously been passed down for generations, for pickling and preserving, or serving up game like muskrat, possum, and woodchuck. Eight different corn pudding recipes are included. There are, of course, nearly 40 recipes featuring crab. The book also weaves prayers throughout, a constant reminder of spirituality and its ties to the kitchen.

My own copy has a previous owner's index of favorite recipes hand-written in the back cover- mostly for some of the cakes. When the compilers of "What is Cooking on Party Line" received multiple submissions of very similar recipes, they attribute the recipe to multiple names. It's interesting to observe the way the recipes had spread and been shared, even before this popular cookbook was published.

I decided to make one of the more 'popular' recipes and so I made "One Hundred Dollar Fudge," a recipe with seven names listed underneath. The corn syrup in the fluff controls sugar crystallization, and my fudge came out so smooth that it got comments on that fact.

William Phillips passed away in November 1994, and the show came to an end. WICO Program Director Dave Parks recalled "he was one of the last local superstars in radio. One of a dying breed. He was known all over the Eastern Shore. He was like a Hollywood star here. He endured because of his personality. He really was Mr. Radio."

Some younger cooks who have inherited copies of the book may have never heard the show, but many people still recall it fondly and can sing the jingle by heart.

"Hello.

Is this the party line?

Yes, it's your party line and it's time for all the gossip on your party line.

What's goin' on, tell us who, when and how?

Well, just listen in to your party line now.

WICO Radio brings you the latest on your party line, party line." ❊

One Hundred Dollar Fudge

2 sticks margarine or butter
4 1/2 c. sugar
1 can evaporated milk
Cook over medium high heat and bring to a rapid
boil, stirring constantly. Boil exactly five minutes,
remove from heat and add:
3 c. (18 oz.) chocolate chips
9 oz. jar marshmallow creme
Stir until melted. Add:
2 Tbsp. vanilla
1/2 c. nuts
1 c. peanut butter (optional)
Pour into buttered 13x9 inch baking pan. Set in
refrigerator overnight. Then set out two hours before
cutting or it will crumble. Makes 5 lbs. of fudge.

Recipe from "What Is Cooking On Party Line," Broad Creek Printing, 1983

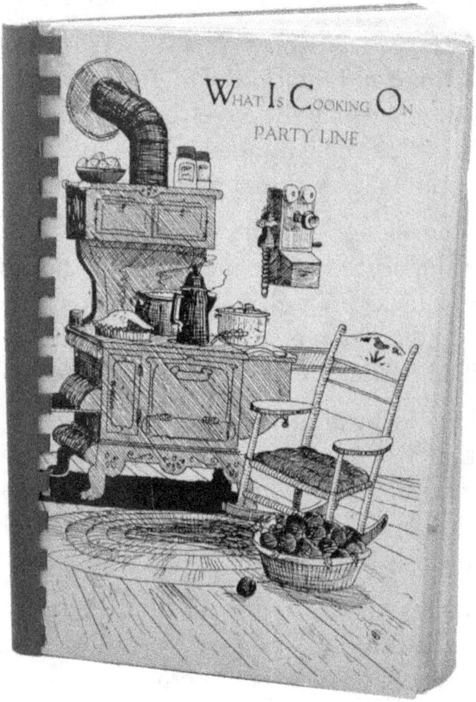
WHAT IS COOKING ON
PARTY LINE

Queen of Oude Sauce

Posted on October 27, 2023

"At the funeral of the Queen of Oude, a diadem was placed on her brow," read a story in the Baltimore Daily Exchange in 1858. The short report, filed under "Foreign Miscellany," focused on jewels, describing "a necklace of lapiz lazuli round her neck, and circlets of amber round her arms and legs. A number of amulets were also attached to the covering in which her body was enveloped."

Throughout Europe and the United States, newspapers reported on the Paris funeral, which the Fayetteville Semi-Weekly Observer in North Carolina dubbed "a rare spectacle for the pageant-loving population of that great metropolis."

"The crowd of curious spectators was so great that it was almost impossible for the procession to move along," the Observer observed. For years afterward, fashion columns reported that ladies in Paris and London emulated the tasseled silk scarves worn by Malika Kishwar, the last Queen of Oude.

The story of how Kishwar ended up dying in Paris, to be buried in the world-famous Père Lachaise cemetery along with Chopin, Oscar Wilde, and Jim Morrison, is a rather sad footnote in the story of British colonialism in India. Obviously, that history is too involved for my little food blog.

Located in the present-day region of Uttar Pradesh, Oude (alternately spelled Oudh, Avadh, or Awadh) was a princely state in India, meaning it wasn't directly ruled by the British. When enab Aliya Begum aka Malika Kishwar was born in the city of Lucknow, around 1805, the British were in the business of intervening to appoint government officials, and demanding revenue from the kingdom, while also gradually placing regions of the state under more direct rule.

In 1847, Kishwar's son Wajid (also spelled Wahid) Ali Shah ascended to the throne as King of Awadh. The East India Company was eager to annex the throne. Stories of the King being a "debauched and detached" ruler circulated. They were possibly British propaganda. Wajid Ali Shah is depicted in some accounts as generous, compassionate, devout in prayer, and a patron of the arts and literature. Nonetheless, the East India Company used the pretense of "bad governance" to take over in 1856, exiling the King to Calcutta. This unscrupulous move is cited as one of the main reasons for the Indian uprising of 1857.

When Wahid Ali Shah fell ill and was unable to make the trip to London to plead his case to be reinstated to the throne, Malika Kishwar stepped in.

Newspapers reported with fascination on the Queen, who traveled with a large entourage, including family members and many servants carrying drapery to seclude the queen from public view as per their religious custom.

When Kishwar finally got an audience with the Queen of England, she realized that Queen Victoria queen wasn't particularly politically involved and that the matter should be pleaded before Parliament. According to a story by Jack Wilson for the Daily Echo in 2021, her petition was dismissed "on the grounds that she had not used the required word "humble", before the word "petition", and the word "humbly", before the word "pray."

To add insult to injury, Malika Kishwar was denied the right to return home unless she declared herself a British subject. Rather than submit to this humiliation, she headed home via France. In January of 1858 she died and was buried in Paris. In February, the Baltimore Sun reported that "it is said that the Queen of Oude died of grief... The prayers enjoined by the Buddhist religion were said over her death-bed." This is probably a confusion with Muslim customs.

The name "Queen of Oude Sauce" may have given an air of exoticism to this recipe, which likely originated around the time of Kishwar's trip to London and subsequent death. The sauce contains generous quantities of cinnamon, cloves, and allspice. The horseradish was a giveaway that this is not an Indian sauce. I confirmed as much with Nandita Godbole, author of many Indian cookbooks and the Curry Cravings Kitchen Blog. "The cider vinegar and horseradish are not old-fashioned Indian ingredients," she confirmed, "I think this recipe is likely an alteration of something more local to Paris."

I don't know how popular this sauce actually was, but I did find a reference to it in a 1930 newspaper, The Morning News in Wilmington Delaware, which ran a column called "Pertinent Questions" by W.H. Hill. "Who was the Queen Oude after an old-time sauce was named?," asked Hill, before positing how tourists' money melts like snow, and some confusing joke about spinsters. Kishwar had been forgotten.

Jane Gilmor Howard included a recipe in her 1873 book "Fifty Years in a Maryland Kitchen," for "Veritable Oude Sauce Or Chetney (From An Old English Receipt Book)." Hers is a more Indian-inspired mix of onions, tomatoes, a small amount of salt fish, and lots of chili peppers.

Recipes similar to the one I used appeared in newspapers and cookbooks in the 1880s. This one was clipped into a scrapbook compiled by a member of Baltimore's Merganthaler family in the early 1900s. The document was shared with me by Joyce White, who acquired the notebook for the Maryland State Archives earlier this year.

At its inception, the sauce was surely not so much about honoring Malika Kishwar than about ignorant fascination with the seemingly exotic and foreign. It's interesting how novel she apparently was to average people in England and the United States, even after centuries of the East India Company extracting wealth and resources from India. For everyday people, it was an invisible and remote influence other than a cup of tea and maybe some spices.

Still, here we are. I've now spent hours reading about the East India Company and the Oudh State and the Indian Rebellion of 1857. I've also enjoyed this sauce on fish, burgers, and meatballs. And I've learned about the life of Malika Kishwar, Queen of Oude... who probably never tasted horseradish in her life. May she rest in peace. ❀

Grape Ketchup.

Take 5 pounds of ripe Concord grapes picked from stem, wash, mash, put in preserving kettle and boil for few minutes. Mash again and strain, pressing through the strainer with spoon as much of the pulp as possible. Boil the juice with 2½ pounds sugar, 2 cups cider vinegar, 1 teaspoonful each of cloves, cinnamon and allspice. Boil for two hours, bottle and seal. This is delicious served with cold lamb or pork.

MRS. E. R. J.,
North Calvert street.

Chili Sauce.

One peck of tomatoes skinned chopped fine, 2 cupfuls of green sweet peppers, 2 cups of onions, all through a meat-grinder; 2 cups brown or white sugar, 3 tablespoonfuls of salt, 2 pints of good vinegar, 2 teaspoons each of cloves, cinnamon and allspice, 2 teaspoons of ginger level tablespoons of celery seed, small lemon, cut fine; boil for 2 hours and seal white hot. Add sufficient red pepper to suit taste.

This recipe is an exceedingly good one, the lemon giving just an added flavor.

MRS. L. M. T.,
Barclay street

Peter Piper's Pepper Sauce.

The "bell" pepper has come to be

Queen of Oude Sauce

"One peck of sound green tomatoes, 6 green sweet peppers (big ones), 48 onions (silver skins), 2 cupfuls each of salt, sugar and freshly grated horseradish, 2 tablespoonfuls each of ground cloves, allspice and cinnamon. Chop the tomatoes very fine, sprinkle the salt over them and let them stand all night. In the morning pour off the liquid, chop the onions and peppers very fine, mix into the tomatoes, add the sugar, horseradish and spices, and stir all well together. Then put into a kettle, cover with cider vinegar and let it boil slowly until well cooked, thick and tender. Will take several hours, but the best test is the tenderness of the vegetables— must be "cooked to rags." Bottle and seal while hot or put in small jars."

Recipe from Merganthaler Recipe Scrapbook, c 1920s, Maryland State Archives

Ripe Tomato Sauce.

Cabbage Chutney.

Green Tomato Sauce.

Cut up 2 gallons of green tomatoes and run through a food chopper; then add 2 gills black mustard seed, 3 tablespoons salt, 3 tablespoons dry mustard, 2½ tablespoons black pepper, 1½ tablespoons allspice, 2 tablespoons celery seed, 1 pound granulated sugar, 1 quart chopped onions, 2½ quarts good vinegar, a little red pepper to taste. Boil all together until well done, then let it cool off a little and put in pint jars. I have been making this sauce for eight years and never had any spoil on me. I have had it keep for two years and the older it gets the better it tastes. onions rather coarsely and mince the garlic. Cook these three ingredients with the salt, sugar and vinegar until soft, and press them through a fine hair sieve; add the raisins, which have been quartered, the ginger thinly sliced, the cayenne pods crushed and the mustard seed. Mix well together and pour into a jar and stand in a warm, but not too hot, place until next morning. Then put the mixture in a dry, wide-mouthed bottle or bottles. Make airtight. This will keep for

One peck ripe tomatoes; scald, and cut small. One quart vinegar (best cider), 1 ounce ground allspice, one ounce white mustard seed, one half ounce celery seed, one quart onions chopped fine, a little horse-radish (if desired), one pound granulated sugar and six large red peppers, all in a preserving kettle and let three hours. Pack in large-mouth bottles and seal. This is a splendid sauce.

MRS. C. C. U.,
Fremont avenue

Queen Of Oude Sauce

Chutney.

Cold Ketchup.

One-half peck ripe tomatoes; and cut them fine, then put through a colander, and add two roots grated horse-radish, one teacup of salt, teaspoon black and white mustard seed, three large red peppers chopped fine, two teaspoons celery seed, cup of onions chopped fine, one spoon ground cloves, one teaspoon ground mace, one cup brown sugar, one teaspoon ground cinnamon, one quart vinegar; mix well together and bottle.

MRS. J. S. S.,
North Calhoun street

Embutido, Thelma Magturo

Posted on October 24, 2019

Thelma Magturo was barely a year old when Japan attacked the Commonwealth of the Philippines in December, 1941. The United States had been transitioning the Philippine Islands to independence in a process drawn out over the preceding decades. In 1936 the U.S. had provided some funds to establish the Philippine Army. Facing growing concerns about Japan's invasion of China and alignment with the Axis Powers, President Franklin D. Roosevelt issued orders calling the Philippine troops into service for the United States in July of 1941.

By most accounts, the Philippine Army had been ill-equipped and poorly trained. Many of the troops did not speak the same languages. They were given old rifles, flimsy shoes, and insufficient quantities of helmets, gas masks, blankets, and other tools. Despite all this, Roosevelt asked the Filipinos to stand with the U.S. and fight alongside U.S. troops under Gen. Douglas MacArthur. Roosevelt restated the United States' commitment to full independence for the Commonwealth.

In January of 1942, the Japanese army occupied Manila. Roosevelt ordered General MacArthur to withdraw in February. Filipino locals continued to resist the Japanese occupation. More than a million were killed. The U.S. would return in 1944 to fight until Japan's surrender in August of 1945.

Thelma Magturo's father, Major Dr. Jose Daluz Estrella, was one of the Filipino veterans of the war.

It was not just the events of the war, but the aftermath which would affect the course of Thelma Magturo's life. In 1946, the U.S. Congress passed legislation to strip veteran recognition from the 250,000 people who'd fought with the U.S. They were even denied their right to become naturalized citizens.

In the 1990s, Magturo joined demonstrations and forums advocating for justice for Filipino World War II veterans. According to one obituary, "She provided rides and refreshments and was a constant presence at public forums and protest actions."

Magturo worked with the American Coalition for Filipino Veterans, an organization that has gradually received some concessions from Congress, such as citizenship rights and some benefit payouts. Meanwhile, the numbers of the surviving World War II veterans have dwindled.

For Thelma Magturo, this work was a way to honor her father. "When I am with the veterans I feel that Papa is always on my side," she said.

Magturo was also a passionate promoter of Filipino culture, teaching folk dance and organizing cultural events. Based on her obituaries from April 2019, she was a lively character who faced her terminal cancer diagnosis with an inspirational amount of courage.

"On November 5, 2017, Thelma posted a picture of herself on Facebook riding a mechanical bull, with this note: 'At 77, a Filipina cowgirl. Hee Haw. I did it. Enjoy, today is the first day of my life. I live one day at a time. Every day is a new day to start and I like to explore. God be with us always and guide us through.' The sign at the entrance to the bullpen said: 'Ride at your own risk.'" – Thelma V. Estralla obituary, inquirer.net

Thelma's recipe for "Embutido," a sort of stuffed meatloaf, appears in the 1973 "Rosemary Hills International Community Cookbook" from Silver Spring Maryland. The book reflects the foodways of the DC-area I grew up in, with recipes for Peanut Stew from Ghana, Barfi from India, Arroz con Pescado from Guatemala, Gefilte Fish, and Chicken Nuggets.

Magturo declared that her Embutido goes good with ketchup, so I took the opportunity to use a beloved Filipino condiment: spicy banana ketchup.

I'm not the best at understanding war, let alone writing about it. I was very touched by Thelma's obituaries so hopefully I have done some justice to an issue that was important to her. I know I learned about a lot more than food. Once again. ❊

Embutido

1 kilogram ground pork
2 chorizo or native sausage, sliced
3 hard-boiled & sliced egg
1 raw egg
sweet, sliced pickle
4 Tablespoon flour
or broth stock
pepper, black
salt

Put together pork, raw egg, flour, salt and pepper to taste. Mix well. On cheese cloth, spread this mixture and on it arrange pickles, hard boiled eggs and chorizo or sausage. Roll mixture into shape and wrap. Tie at both ends. Place in deep pan, cover with broth and simmer until done. When cooked, remove from fire and chill in refrigerator. Unwrap before serving. Slice. Catsup goes very well with this.

Recipe from "Rosemary Hills International Community Cookbook," compiled by Gwendolyn Coffield and Juanita Hamby, 1973

Portuguese Sweet Bread Sgt. Mercedes Rankin

Posted on March 4, 2016

When Mercedes V. Rankin shared her recipe for "Portuguese Sweet Bread" in the "Bethel Cookbook", assembled by the parish of the historic Bethel A.M.E. in 1979, she probably hoped to do her part to raise money for her church.

What she surely did not know is that some random weirdo would bake this bread 36 years later, search her name and uncover stories from her past and other ways she strove to make a difference.

Mercedes Rankin, I learned, was one of the first female police officers put "on the beat" in Baltimore.

Born Mercedes Rawlings in 1933, Rankin joined the Baltimore City Police Department in 1960. In 1968 she married fellow police officer Donald O. Rankin.

Mercedes Rankin appears to have been an involved officer, engaging with community groups, working with troubled youth and the elderly, and in 1969 receiving a citation for her work developing a block mothers program to aid children in need.

In 1973, when the BCPD ended the policy of discrimination based on gender, Mercedes became one of the first two officers put on the beat, along with Sergeant Bessie Norris, who was in the Narcotics division.

"They won't last a day," said one male member of the force when told of the change. – 'Sex Distinction Ended in Police Hiring, Duties', Baltimore Sun, 1973

Baltimore had its share of turmoil in the 1970s. Mercedes Rankin was assigned to patrol a troubled area in the Northwestern District. In 1977, one of the youth she worked with after school was slain before he could testify in a robbery case. "Tony was just a charming little fellow," she said of the young man.

Rankin seems to have reacted to her promotion humbly and in stride.

"Sergeant Rankin said yesterday she is not frightened by her high-crime-area assignment. "I think I can handle myself. I feel like I'm one of the boys," she said. "Once more women are assigned, they'll be accepted." – 'Sex Distinction Ended in Police Hiring, Duties', Baltimore Sun, 1973

One of the most telling insights into the character of Mercedes Rankin is a letter she wrote to the Baltimore Sun in 1965 in apparent response to Rev. Marion Bascom making a quip about police getting "kick-backs":

"Officers Catania and Osborne... practically gave their lives to save the lives of seven small children. Did they get kick backs?...

Violet Hill Whyte... has done little else but worry about Baltimore's people and their problems...

If police are receiving kick-backs and Bascom has knowledge of this, why doesn't he become a better citizen and report it to the proper authorities?

Mr. Bascom should go into the districts and see an officer receive a smile from the people he helps. This is his kick-back, his reward, and that smile is far more precious than any kick-back he could ever receive. Take it from one who knows."

Note how she champions the accomplishments of others. At least in the press, Rankin didn't make much of her groundbreaking status, the apparent empathy and outreach that she brought to the position, nor to the fact that she was promoted to sergeant 11 months before her husband Donald.

At the time when Mercedes Rankin contributed her recipe to the Bethel Cookbook, the pastor would have been John Richard Bryant, who is credited with reviving the church and growing the congregation.

Dating back to 1785, Bethel African Methodist Episcopal Church (Bethel A.M.E.) Baltimore is the oldest independent continuously operating African American church in the state of Maryland.

According to Wikipedia: "Portuguese sweet bread is common in both Hawaiian cuisine and New England cuisine as it was brought to those regions by their large Portuguese immigrant populations." This sweet bread recipe was traditionally baked around the Easter holiday.

Rankin's recipe didn't specify whether the butter should be melted, and the internet seems to go either way. I went with melted butter and this turned out fine. I was worried by how dark the crust became in the oven but after I let it sit and cut it open, it yielded a delicious sweet snack. I enjoyed it with lime curd, and later used it to make excellent French toast.

Mercedes Rankin passed away in September of 2011. According the Baltimore Police Department website:

"Hundreds of women currently serve on the Baltimore Police Department. Female police officers serve as detectives, sergeants, lieutenants, and members of the command staff in a variety of assignments within the department. There are NO assignments that a female can't do or isn't open to, including police commissioner." ✿

Portuguese Sweet Bread

2 package yeast
.25 Cup lukewarm water
1 Cup sugar
1 Teaspoon salt
6 Cup regular flour
3 eggs, beaten
1 Cup milk
1 stick butter, melted
Start yeast in small bowl in lukewarm water with a pinch of sugar, until mixture begins to bubble and rise. Combine remaining sugar, salt and 4 cups of the flour in a large bowl. Make a well in the middle and drop in the eggs, yeast mixture and milk. Mix with spoon. Add butter and more flour and knead in with hands. Gradually add enough flour until dough can be shaped into a big soft ball and begins to pull away from sides of bowl when mixed. Knead until dough becomes smooth, shiny and rubbery. Cover with damp cloth and allow to rise until doubled in size (about one hour). Punch dough down and allow to "rest" 10 minutes. Shape into two loaves, place on baking sheet(s). Let loaves rise again about 45 minutes. Preheat oven to 350°. Place loaves on top rack of oven. Bake about 45 minutes to one hour – until crusts are golden brown. If desired, brush top of loaves with egg yolk mixed with water after baking for about 30 minutes. Allow to cool before slicing. Makes 2 loaves.

Recipe adapted from Bethel Cookbook, contributed by parishioner Mercedes V. Rankin

---

Bethel Cookbook

Bethel A.M.E. Church
Druid Hill Avenue and Lanvale Street
Baltimore, Maryland
1979

Martha Washington Cake, Dutch Tea Room

Posted on January 12, 2018

"And so we are really going to have a tea room after all; it is to be a perfect love of a place, all little blue and white China teacups, and walls papered in cunning blue figures, and the name of this delicate place of amusement is going to be the 'Dutch Tea Room.' If you have happened to go to Baltimore, or visit Baltimore, or have friends who have, why you know all about the little tea room there that has the same name and has – been run by society girls for the past several years." – The Times Dispatch, Richmond, VA, 1912

In 1907, Harriet Stanton Blatch met her friend Hettie Wright Graham for dinner. The destination was the famous Hoffman House hotel in New York. The "palace hotel" was known for fine food, expensive artwork, celebrity guests, and rye whiskey. Blatch and Graham took the elevator up to the fashionable rooftop garden dining area but were denied a table. The owner told Blatch that women diners were not allowed without a male escort. The policy was meant to protect women such as Blatch and Graham from having to dine near "objectionable" women. "When I have been annoyed it has been by men," Blatch remarked. "I do not suppose you make any effort to keep objectionable men out." She attempted to sue the hotel, and lost.

In the decades after the Civil War, a glamorous new era of restaurant dining was emerging. It wasn't considered respectable for women to dine without male accompaniment in these places.

At the same time, women were spending more time outside of the home, whether it was working, shopping, or socializing. In "Ten Restaurants That Changed America", author Paul Freedman wrote that "the period from 1890 to 1910 saw the proliferation of many types of middle-class restaurants, ranging from those featuring Chinese and other foreign cuisines to tearooms, coffee shops, cafeterias, and other inexpensive but orderly places to have lunch. These were not necessarily intended exclusively for women, but the fact that they did not serve alcohol made them seem appropriate places for unaccompanied women to dine." (Note: Some accounts claim that it wasn't always tea in those ladies' teapots!) These types of establishments offered up "decorous but economical refuge, a midday oasis of sorts, where women who were shopping could dine and recuperate, or where women who worked in offices or stores could have a tranquil if more hurried lunch."

A 1904 article in The Carlisle Pennsylvania Sentinel advised that opening a tea room was "a profitable occupation for women," as long as the woman had "a business head and [knew] how to count up profit and loss" as well as experience "making all kinds of cakes in the best homemade way."

Baltimore was the 6th-largest city in the United States around this time, and had a number of tea rooms. The most famous and enduring is the tea room in the Women's Exchange. Department stores like Hutzler's had a tea room inside the store. The Parkway Theater on North Avenue had a tea room which was "swarmed" with people waiting for the second showing of films each day. In the segregated city there was also at least one Black-owned tea room – "The Little Gem" in Sandtown on Robert Street.

In 1914, author Julian Street came to Baltimore and visited the Women's Exchange where he encountered a "great numbers of ladies sitting upon tall stools and eating at a lunch-counter." He described the sight as "a somewhat curious spectacle, perhaps, but neither pleasing to the eye nor thrilling to the senses."

In the mid-19th century, American society began to develop the stereotype that women preferred different kinds of foods than men. Delmonico steak might be alright for men, but women require something "daintier" – things like cakes, fruit, salads, and egg dishes.

"The development of dining-out options for women was accompanied by a growing sense that women had their own preferences and could, at least in the company of other ladies, indulge them. The obvious advantage of all-female lunches was that women could partake of what they actually liked to eat." – Ten Restaurants That Changed America

The tea rooms became a place not just for socializing but for politics including suffrage and prohibition. The Southern Tea Room at 206 Park Avenue hosted lectures on women's suffrage and greeted suffragette Alice Paul with a reception in 1910.

Marguerite Schertle was a tea room waitress for nearly 80 years. At age 92 she was profiled in "Maryland's Vanishing Lives" where she shared the memories of tea room culture, where the customers were known by name as "Miss this and Miss that," desserts like butterscotch and charlotte russe were still served, and where oftentimes sisters were employed side by side. Her own sister "Miss Anna" had worked with her at the Women's Exchange until her death in 1992. The women had even married "look-alike" brothers and started families in adjacent bungalows in Hamilton. Schertle passed away in 2001 at 100 years old.

Before her half-century-long tenure at the Women's Exchange, Schertle had worked for 20 years across the street at the Dutch Tea Room at 314 N. Charles.

The Dutch Tea Room had been opened in 1904 by Natalie Cole, who was, according to the Baltimore Sun, a "lady of social standing." The popular tea room was even visited by President Wilson – almost. In 1913 he stopped by with his family but the place was too crowded so they went to the Rennert instead. Cole still got to serve her country in 1917, when the tea room baked 300 "extra fine" fruit cakes for soldiers at Camp Meade.

In 1918 Natalie Cole married William Wilson Galbreath, who is listed in some directories as a salesman of "porcelain products." Hmm. Cole and her husband passed away in 1959 and 1952, respectively. I'm not sure when the Dutch Tea Room actually closed for business.

According to the Baltimore Sun obituary for Marguerite Schertle, when she'd worked at the Dutch Tea Room she had baked "Lady Baltimore, orange and Wellesley fudge cakes."

I don't have recipes for those cakes but I found a recipe in an undated, unpublished manuscript for a "Martha Washington Cake," attributed to the Dutch Tea Room. The cake is actually a predecessor to Boston Creme Pie, with a custard filling and minus the chocolate topping. Although Boston Creme Pie has been sometimes called "Washington Pie" (or Cake), the Martha name is rarer – it's typically known as a "Martha Washington Cream Pie." The name is obviously more dainty and befitting a tea room.

Early 20th century menus suggest that both a cup of tea and a slice of cake would run about fifteen cents – $1.92 in today's money. At that price, I could go for a tea room lunch. Myself and most dainty ladies would be quick to notice that it leaves more money and appetite for a burger and a beer for dinner. Male accompaniment optional, thanks. ❀

Martha Washington Cake - Dutch Tea Room

Cake:
1/2 cup sugar
1/2 cup flour
3 eggs
Beat yolks then add the sugar. Fold in stiffly beaten whites, then gently fold in flour, stirring as little as possible. Bake in one cake tin. (A smaller taller cake might be preferable to the 9 inch tin I used.)

Filling:
1 cup milk
1 egg
1/2 cup sugar
1/4 cup flour
vanilla to taste
Scald the milk. Beat flour, sugar and egg in a separate bowl then mix in 1/4 to 1/2 cup of the scalded milk. Return to pan and cook over medium heat until thickened. Cool thoroughly.
Split the cake vertically and spread filling in the middle. Top with powdered sugar.

Recipe Adapted from "Cookbook of Maryland and Virginia Recipes" manuscript in the American Antiquarian Society collection.

Jelly Roll No. 2, "Timely Tips for Bakers"

Posted on July 24, 2022

"Baltimore's rapid industrial progress is being reflected in growth of population... Allowing this city an annual increase of 16,500 the 800,000 mark will be passed during 1924. Apparently the 1,000,000 mark will be reached at the time of the next census in 1930." — George C. Smith, director of the Baltimore Board of Trade's Industrial Bureau, to the Evening Sun in May 1923

At first glance, "Timely Tips for Bakers" looks like any other corporate cookbook aimed at housewives. On the front of the tall thin brochure-sized booklet, a uniformed man holds up a perfect layer cake. The first page features a photograph of the headquarters of "The International Company," producers of ingredients like "Velvet Egg" and "Eggrowhite" powdered egg products, Sunrise Baking Powder, and "Mex-Val-Ol" vanilla flavoring. Recipes, of course, can be found within.

On closer inspection the recipes call for two and three pounds of flour at a time for cakes and cookies. When I baked the recipe for "Jelly Roll No. 2," I had to get out a calculator.

The ample text in the cookbook, most of which extols the benefits of the International Company's product offerings, also contains some information about the School of Commercial Cake Baking, an experimental bakery where professional bakers from around the country were encouraged to visit to receive instruction in the latest technology and best techniques of cake baking. Presumably, the bakers were encouraged to familiarize themselves with the company's product line.

In other words, "Timely Tips for Bakers" is meant literally. This is not a book full of tempting cakes for church suppers.

The origins of "The International Company" lie with the Pitt Brothers company, started by Pembroke W. & Clarence M. Pitt in the 19th century. The brothers were grain merchants. Business went on quietly for a few decades. On November 4th, 1911, the Sun announced "GRAIN FIRM FAILS." Failure is a rather generous way of stating it. The story went on to say that Pembroke W. Pitt had forged bills of lading in order to defraud local banks of over $500,000. Adjusted for inflation, that is almost fifteen million dollars.

Pembroke Pitt proceeded to leave the city, leaving Clarence confused (or feigning confusion). Debtors attempted to collect money or wheat that they were owed, and the police began a search. The press began ramping up the coverage. As the inquiry continued, a very guilty-seeming Pitt was reported seen in Philadelphia with his mustache shaved off, purchasing a ticket to head south. On the 5th, his wife Nettie was allegedly missing from their Roland Park home. Friends expressed shock that the seemingly frugal and free-of-vice Pembroke Pitt had dug himself such a hole. The search continued.

A few days later, police detective Thomas M. Hogan was sent on Pembroke's trail. At home, Clarence was expelled from the Chamber of Commerce. The papers salivated at the idea that Pitt could commit suicide if he were cornered by police. They covered the little details they had of Detective Hogan's "mysterious mission" to track down Pembroke Pitt. By the 12th, the Baltimore Sun reported that "police are still at sea about much-wanted grain man." The police failure was becoming the story. Hogan returned to Baltimore, claiming to have been on vacation.

On December 5th, Mrs. Pitt returned to Baltimore. Despite having disappeared the prior month around the same time as her husband, Mrs. Pitt now claimed to have no knowledge of his whereabouts or his crimes. She stayed with friends in order to avoid the press frenzy waiting at her home.

On the 10th, rumors circulated that the lights had come on in the Pitt home. A figure was seen moving about in the house – a figure suspected to be Pembroke in women's clothing. Apparently, Pitt had been involved in theater in his younger days and "made quite a success as a female impersonator," ie what we would now call a drag queen.

The holidays arrived and the Sun headline read "WHERE IS MR. PITT?" reporting on the growing cost of the police search for him. By the end of the year, some of the defrauded banks offered

$100 for information leading to his capture. The estimated amount of funds he had stolen was also significantly reduced to $200,000.

In April 1912, Pitt's home at 411 Forest Road was reportedly sold.

In May, he was located in Greece. The Sun printed a map of his pursuit, which took police through the Caribbean, across the Atlantic Ocean, and through the strait of Gibraltar. Pitt was arrested in Italy on May 8th.

Pitt was sentenced to five years in prison but was pardoned by Governor Phillips Lee Goldsborough two years later, because Pitt's family made restitution.

Clarence continued in the business, forming a baking supply company called "C.M. Pitt and Sons," with his son Clarence B. (1892-1946).

It's hard to pick through these companies' histories, but there was some type of merger with "The Cabell Company", which had been founded by Frederick Mortimer Cabell (1883-1957). Cabell's father had been a grain merchant. He is listed in the 1910 census as the manager of a "baking supply" company and in 1930 the manager of a "food products" company. He and his wife Bessie lived at 2834 Maryland Avenue in the Charles Village neighborhood.

A 1918 industry paper referencing the International Company notes that it was "formerly the Cabell Company." In 1924, the Cabell Company – still named as such- was acquired by the "Joe Lowe Co.," of New York – then the largest importers of dried egg. Another trade document lists C. M. Pitt & Sons as a subsidiary of the Cabell Company.

A 1916 trade document mentioned many representatives who'd attended a baking convention. Representing the Cabell Co: F. M. Cabell, R. T. Hicks... and the presumably-rehabilitated P. W. Pitt.

I researched many of the different names that came up in relation to these corporations. R.T. Hicks wrote impassioned letters to the Sun defending the baking industry and the high cost of bread.

Chemist William S. Arnold (1897-1965) was also a big player in the Pitt/Cabell/International Company. He worked for the Pitt Company for 40 years, eventually becoming its vice president in 1951.

The gist of the International Company's contribution to food history is that someone figured out it was cheaper to import dried eggs from China than to purchase fresh eggs domestically. "Timely Tips for Bakers" calls for many of their flavorings and products, but the Velvet Egg seems to really be the driving force.

In 1920, C. M. Pitt was accused by the government of adulterating one of their products, Eggrowhite. The company countersued for defamation but lost. In 1927 the company's warehouse at the corner of Exchange Pl and Commerce was conveyed to real-estate broker Walter Pugh.

I assume that was the end of the International Company.

C. M. Pitt & Sons kept right on through the 1960s, producing ice cream products. They were embroiled in a few more government cases involving adulteration in the 1930s. It seems they finally went under in the early 70s, unable to keep up with the big national brands.

In 1925, the year after acquiring the Cabell Company, the New-York-based Joe Lowe Company acquired the Popsicles brand from its inventor, who had been sued by Good Humor for his invention and was broke and dejected. Joe Lowe Company grew the Popsicle brand, and eventually they were acquired by the Good Humor Company in 1989. The Good Humor Company was acquired by Unilever, who also acquired Breyers in 1993 and merged the brands (and, sadly, ruined all the Breyers products – someone should investigate THEM for adulteration.)

This all makes me wonder if the influence of chemist William S. Arnold, working for the Pitt/Cabell/International Company, isn't still with us in a way. Maybe that "Eggrowhite" grew into a supply used to make toaster strudels or something. Perhaps "Mex-Val-Ol" is behind the taste of a vanilla wafer. I may never know, and the recipe didn't get me any closer to knowing.

Although I can't procure "Velvet Egg" or "Velvet Milk," I used powdered milk. I attempted to find dried egg, but it turns out that dehydrated egg is kind of expensive. I had to get out my calculator once again. The resulting jelly roll was, unsurprisingly, a failure. I did my best to redeem it by turning it into more of a jelly layered cake.

Pembroke's journey around the world, and the newspaper's enthralled coverage of it is only tangential to the International Company, but I had too much fun reading about it to not write about it. It's a reminder that behind the rise and fall of Baltimore's industrial age, there were people with stories. People whose financial ambitions changed the way we eat. Some may have had epic falls from grace. Most just retired quietly and left their eponymous companies to be merged into a Unilever oblivion. ❊

Jelly Roll No. 2

Rub up by hand:
1 pt. Dissolved Velvet Egg
1 1/2 lbs. Sugar
2 ozs. Velvet Milk (dry)
Salt
Flavor
Now Mix in:

1 pt. Water
Now sieve together and then rub in by hand until smooth:
2 1/4 lbs. Winter Flour
1 1/2 ozs. Sunrise Baking Powder
Bake at 425 degrees F.

Recipe from "Timely Tips for Bakers," Sixth Issue, The International Company, 1922

Delmonico's Pudding & Delmonico Potatoes

Posted on January 26, 2020

Although Maryland's history of celebrated restaurants, hotels and caterers may have influenced the cuisine that we enjoy to this day, there are very few recipes that can be directly tied to the early chefs.

Chefs tended to work more intuitively and from experience. Recipes – even the relatively vague ones found in 19th-century cookbooks, simply weren't necessary.

By the time Frederick Phillip Stieff and others began to transcribe and collect recipes from famed establishments, a generation of Baltimore caterers had come and gone.

Instead, that legacy is woven throughout the recipes collected by well-to-do housewives and circulated in church cookbooks, eventually passing traces of restaurant prestige into everyday meals.

The name of one specific restaurant does appear in many Maryland recipe manuscripts, church and corporate cookbooks alike, and is not a Maryland restaurant at all.

New York as a restaurant hub may seem like a given to us today, but when John and Peter Delmonico opened a pastry shop there in 1827, New York was not at all considered a cultural capital or refined place. The growing city was a hub of trade with occasional rioting and fires. A growing class of newly wealthy merchants mingled with "old money" to provide Delmonico's with a steady clientele.

It was Lorenzo Delmonico who is credited with building the Delmonico's empire into a stalwart of fine dining that reigned over the gilded age. Lorenzo arrived from Switzerland to join his uncle's growing business in 1831. Other Delmonico family members quickly followed, but Lorenzo had an outsized influence on the restaurant, and by extension, American dining.

Delmonico's is credited with being one of the first restaurants in America to offer a la carte dining instead of a fixed menu. Lorenzo as manager created an atmosphere where diners enjoyed luxurious and leisurely meals. The allure proved hard to resist, despite a prevailing American culture of "mistrust" for snobbery and "Old World vices."

Harpers weekly referred to Delmonico's as an "agency of civilization" in 1884. The restaurant was visited by many of the admired figures who visited the U.S. in the 19th century, including Charles Dickens, Oscar Wilde, and Jenny Lind, who allegedly dined there after each of her New York shows.

In 1871, Grand Duke Alexis of Russia visited the United States and was honored with a lavish meal at Delmonico's. Head Chef Charles Ranhofer produced a twelve-course menu for the event, primarily composed of fine French food, including a special consommé of his own invention. Although the menu was dominated by French cuisine, Terrapin à la Maryland and canvasback duck also made an appearance. If patriotic Maryland cooks couldn't resist the prestige of Delmonico's, perhaps the feeling was mutual.

Ranhofer, who immigrated from France, was a third-generation chef, trained in French kitchens from adolescence. He was hired to work at Delmonico's in 1862. Unlike many of his contemporary chefs and caterers, he didn't see a need to be reserved with his recipes and techniques. In 1893 he produced "The Epicurean", a cookbook of over 3700 recipes plus a record of past menus (including the meal served to Duke Alexis), advice on procuring seasonal produce, plus illustrations of elaborate table settings and kitchen apparatuses. The index alone is 45 pages. Delmonico's manager Leopold Rimmer remarked that Ranhofer had given away all the "secrets of the house."

Ranhofer's book, with its many mother sauces and kitchen equipment illustrations, was written for an audience of culinary professionals. Another Delmonico's chef, Alessandro Filippini, had published a book in 1889 that was geared more towards housewives and home cooks.

In January 2020, I had some friends over and did my best to recreate some of the recipes from both books. I also chose two "Delmonico" recipes from my Maryland cookbooks.

Delmonico potatoes date back to the early days of the restaurant. Essentially escalloped potatoes seasoned with a little nutmeg and sometimes some Parmesan, the potatoes are cut into cubes or sliced, peeled or not. I worked primarily from a recipe from 1888, found in "The Practical Cook Book" by a Baltimore woman named Mrs. J. H. Giese.

Recipes named "Delmonico Pudding" appear in several books spanning the late 1800s through the 1940s. There is a great deal of variation in formula. In the 1900 "Tested Maryland Recipes," a gelatin-based pudding is alternately layered with cherries and macaroons. I opted for a more simple version from 1894, from "Mrs. Charles H. Gibson's Maryland And Virginia Cookbook." Mrs. Gibson's recipe is simply a lightly sweetened vanilla custard made with both eggs and cornstarch, topped with a more highly sweetened meringue.

Unsurprisingly, I was unable to trace these recipes to either Ranhofer or Filippini's books. The most enduring and far-reaching of the recipes from Ranhofer's tome might deserve its own discussion at some point – Lobster A La Newburg. I have 23 recipes for it, spanning the late 1800s up through 1985. We'll save that for another day... and an occasion befitting lobster.

The Delmonico family coincidentally sold their restaurant on the day that Prohibition was enacted. The timing was fitting. Although the business had already been in decline, the inability to bank on alcohol sales spelled the death of the restaurant, which closed its doors in 1923. A later incarnation was opened in 1926 by Oscar Tucci. Tucci's reign was successful, and the restaurant operated in various locations until 1987. Still, even the latter-day recipes in my collection hail from the Ranhofer & Filippini eras. For over a century, home cooks have made and shared these chef's recipes, and in doing so, have kept the Delmonico mystique alive. ❁

Delmonico Potatoes

"Boil the potatoes with skins on. When cold peel, and slice them thin. Put in a shallow pie dish. Scald scant pint of milk with one and a-half tablespoonsful of butter rubbed with the same quantity of flour. Salt, and scald. Pour over the potatoes and bake twenty minutes. They must brown."

Recipe from "The Practical Cook Book," 1888, Mrs. J. H. Giese

Ranhofer & Filippini portraits from their respective books

Delmonico's Pudding

"Five eggs, three tablespoonsful of pulverized sugar, two and one-half tablespoons of corn starch, two and one-half pints of sweet milk. Beat the eggs and sugar very light, leaving out three whites for the meringue. Stir in the corn starch; have the milk on boiling, and while it is boiling stir in the mixture very rapidly. By the time it is all in it will be done; pour into your pudding dish, and put in the stove a minute. Add six tablespoons of pulverized sugar to the three whites, one-half teaspoon of vanilla, and beat to a stiff icing. Beat it in a bowl, and put it on the pudding, and brown it lightly. Add one teaspoonful of vanilla to the pudding before baking it. Let it get very cold and serve it with cold cream."

Recipe from "Mrs. Charles H. Gibson's Maryland And Virginia Cookbook," 1894, Mrs. Charles H. Gibson

Split Pea Soup, Mrs. Rorer

Posted on February 1, 2017

"Bad cooking is largely responsible for the conditions of our insane asylums, almshouses, prisons and hospitals. Bad cooking not only engenders disease, but is directly provocative of crime, while good cooking is the art of making home a paradise for the breadwinner." – Sarah Tyson Rorer

I recently pulled the holiday ham-hock out of the freezer and sought out a split pea soup recipe. I found one to fit my ingredients in a mysterious 1908 Baltimore book simply entitled "The Church Cook Book." Rather than a community cookbook, "The Church Cook Book" is anonymously compiled, with a preface giving credit to The Baltimore Sun, Harper's Bazar, Miss Ellen L. Duff and Mrs. Sarah Tyson Rorer.

The latter two, I learned, were popular cooking instructors at the time.

As mentioned in the "New Year's Cakes" entry, our friend Elizabeth Ellicott Lea was a student of one of America's first cooking schools, led by Mrs. Elizabeth Goodfellow in the early 1800s. Lea was a fairly well-to-do woman who could afford the luxury of cooking instruction. According to a Goodfellow biography by Becky Libourel Diamond, cooking instruction had become much more affordable by the late 19th century.

"Whereas Goodfellow's concentration was primarily teaching daughters of the wealthy to prepare dinner-party fare, Juliet Corson [of the New York Cooking School] conceived a system of graded levels within cooking schools, providing many more options for potential students of various backgrounds. In addition to the introduction of classes in plain cooking and those for the children of working people, this four-tiered approach also included instruction in fancy cookery." – Mrs. Goodfellow: The Story of America's First Cooking School by Becky Libourel Diamond

The Philadelphia Cooking School opened in 1878 with a similar ethos of making education available to women of different economic levels. One of that school's first students was Sarah Tyson Rorer. Not long after completing the three-month curriculum the Philadelphia Cooking School, Rorer became the school's principal. In 1883, she opened her own cooking school. A decade after that, she appeared at the 1893 World's Fair. "She became a household name," wrote Diamond, "and traveled throughout the country to personally demonstrate cooking techniques to one packed auditorium after another."

Thrift had been a popular theme with Juliet Corson, who penned a pamphlet entitled "Fifteen-Cent Dinners for Workingmen's Families" and distributed it for free. Rorer continued the tradition of instruction on food budgeting, but her passion was nutrition. Her cooking school taught contemporary science on carbohydrates, protein, and sugars. Hospitals consulted her for advice on menus for the infirm. In her demonstrations, she declared that dessert was "unhealthy", "unnecessary", and even "deadly" before making a show of reluctantly demonstrating dishes such as Charlotte Russe with Chocolate Sauce, and admonishing the audience not to recreate such dishes at home. She took to heart an English physician's condemnation of white bread as "the staff of death," and with her own flair for the dramatic, she appropriated the saying.

"In the cooking school we do not especially teach elaborate or highly seasoned dishes; the latter we always guard against. The true principles of economy are taught; together with the proper combinations of foods. In fact, we try to teach what to eat and how to cook it." – Sarah Tyson Rorer

The first cooking school in Baltimore (and possibly all of Maryland) opened in 1885 as an arm of the nursery and children's hospital on Carrolton and Mulberry Streets. According to the Sun, "the lady managers will... endeavor by their personal influence to make the art of cooking honorable and fashionable." The first class was taught by Juliet Corson from the New York cooking school.

Although some schools accepted Black servants, whose education was generally paid by the employer, it wasn't long before Baltimore's Black citizens organized their own school out of the YWCA on Park Avenue & Franklin Street in 1896.

There the schoolwork included "moral and religious training," housekeeping, and sewing. Beyond self-improvement and employment opportunities, it was implied that these skills offered an increased level of independence. It was emphasized that girls would be taught to make their own dresses in a twelve-course series of intensive lessons.

In December 1897, Sarah Tyson Rorer came to Baltimore to lecture at the "Santa Claus Food Show," and espoused her prescient admonition that frying pans were a scourge upon the public health. She provided demonstrarions on salads, fish, and bread. She closed her lecture series with advice on feeding a family on ten cents a day. That's roughly three 2017 dollars. Despite the lesson on thrift, she admonished against the eating of organ meats, deeming it dangerous. To back up her claim, she declared that she had inspected a calf's liver under a microscope and found "the presence of small tumors, of which she counted over thirty."

My split pea soup recipe didn't quite turn out as I anticipated, but maybe I just need instruction on how to make it. I assumed that you do NOT drain the water and I ended up with watery soup and needed to add twice as many peas. After that it was alright. Maybe it's supposed to be watery to save money?

I do believe it provided enough nutriment to keep me out of the insane asylum, at least for now. ❁

Split Pea Soup

.5 Cup split peas
1 Quart cold water
.5 small onion
2 Tablespoon butter
1 Tablespoon flour
1 Teaspoon salt
black pepper
1 to 2 Cups hot milk

Pick over and wash the peas. Soak 8 to 12 hours or over night in cold water. Drain off the water and cook peas and onion in 1 quart of water until soft. Press through a strainer, and add butter and flour cooked together. Add seasoning, and thin with hot water or milk, and reheat. Peas will not soften in salted water, so salt should not be added until they are cooked. A small piece of fat salt pork or a ham-bone may be cooked with the peas, and if so, the butter may be omitted. Lentil soup may be made as directed for split pea soup.

Recipe from "The Church Cook Book," 1908

Sarah Tyson Rorer in 1898

Chop-Chae, Ladies of the Bethel

from "Festive Maryland Recipes"

After the Immigration and Nationality Act of 1965 removed discriminatory barriers to moving to the United States, Maryland gained a new population of Korean-born citizens. Naturally, these newly-minted Marylanders brought their celebrations with them. In the 60s and 70s, newspapers began to report on the festivities. A 1970 Lunar New Year event held at the Korean embassy in Washington, D.C. attracted Korean-born Marylanders from around the state. Helen Giblo, a reporter from the Annapolis Capital, described for readers the galbi and "kimchie, a dish that is a way of life in the Land of Morning Calm." Also served was "dduk guk," Rice Cake Soup - a Korean New Year essential.

The Bethel Korean Presbyterian Church of Baltimore was founded in June of 1979, with a parish made up of seven families. "Everyone was on the same boat, sometimes literally," Pastor Billy Park told the Baltimore Sun in 2002. By then, more than 1,700 people were attending Sunday services at the church.

The "Ladies of the Bethel" did not include a recipe for Rice Cake Soup in their 1986 eponymous cookbook. Perhaps the authors felt that the rice cakes were too difficult to acquire or to make. The recipes in the book often reflect the constraints of limited access to ingredients, and provide a contrast to today's vicinity around the church (which moved to Ellicott City in 1987), an area now strewn with multiple international grocers such as H-Mart.

The book does contain many other traditional recipes, with the intention, as Susan Y. Park, the cookbook chairperson wrote, "to introduce as many Korean recipes as possible to those who are accustomed to Western food."

Japchae is one of the most popular Korean dishes for holidays. The recipe in "Ladies of the Bethel" (spelled in the book as "Chop-Chae"), is clearly written by someone with a love of the dish, and its instructions read almost like a monologue.

"After you fry onion and scallion, do the beef so that the spicy flavor can soak into the meat from the pan. Store cooked ingredients in a large bowl so that you can mix them with the noodle all together. Cut up the noodle crisscross a couple of times with scissors to the desired length. Mix all ingredients in the bowl together and add the seasoning to your liking. Sesame seeds or sesame oil should be added at the end to enhance the flavor. Serve when warm. "

Note the serving suggestions at the end. Although we may never know her name, the recipe's anonymous author commands our attention. As evidenced by an errata sheet at the front of the book with such corrections as "dash of cinnamon" to "½ teaspoon" and "1 tsp salt" to "1½ tsp salt," it was important to the "Ladies of the Bethel" that cookbook users experience the recipes at their very best. ✺

CHOP-CHAE (Noodles with Beef and Vegetables)

1 lb. tender, lean beef	1/4 tsp. pepper
2 sticks carrots	1 T. sesame seeds
3 stalks celery	1 tsp. sesame oil
Mushrooms (fresh, well-drained canned or dried)	1 head onion
8 oz. Dang Myun (Chinese noodles)	4 stalks green scallions
	1 stick fish cake (kamaboku)
	3 T. soy sauce
1/4 tsp. salt	1 T. sugar

Cut up all ingredients in thin finger shapes about 2 inches long and keep them separate. If using dried mushrooms, soak them at least 4 hours before cutting. Soak the noodles in hot water for one-half hour and boil over high heat one minute (it turns clear when cooked); then rinse with cold water thoroughly until it is cold and not sticky. Then drain well. Pan fry (stir-fry) vegetables separately on high heat. Heat the pan with a little bit of oil before putting vegetables in. Sprinkle some salt and pepper while frying. After you fry onion and scallion, do the beef so that the spicy flavor can soak into the meat from the pan. Store cooked ingredients in a large bowl so that you can mix them with the noodle all together. Cut up the noodle crisscross a couple of times with scissors to the desired length. Mix all ingredients in the bowl together and add the seasoning to your liking. Sesame seeds or sesame oil should be added at the end to enhance the flavor. Serve when warm. You can freeze this dish and heat it up in a pan or microwave oven for later usage. The above ingredients will make at least 4 servings. You can buy the noodle, fish cake and dried mushrooms at the Oriental grocery store.

Recipe from Ladies of the Bethel, Women's Fellowship of Bethel Korean Church, (Baltimore/Ellicott City), Morris Press. 1986.

Eggplant Fried in Batter, Alice Brown

Posted on December 1, 2017

"In a very real sense, 'Maryland's Way' is Alice Brown's Way." – Tom Coakley, The Capital, Annapolis, 1975

When I finished reading Michael Twitty's book "The Cooking Gene," I was planning to write a whole blog post about it. I found myself basically at a loss to convey any meaningful context other than simply recommending the book itself. I refer to it as 'part history, part memoir, and part philosophy' – with a good amount of expository information about the actual nature of DNA tests and genealogy.

You may be familiar with Twitty's work as a historian if you are an Old Line Plate reader. When I plumb the 18th and 19th – and even the 20th century recipes – that lay the foundation of Maryland food, I'm constantly faced with the gaping holes in our documented food experience – where enslaved cooks, poor cooks, immigrant and working-class cooks had shaped our collective food history or carved out their own spaces in Maryland food. Sometimes it's lost completely. Sometimes we are able to unearth faint traces of the lives and work of these cooks on census records, property records, and surviving narratives. Occasionally, as in St. Mary's County, we are lucky enough to have situations where citizens and historians acted to preserve these stories for the future.

Ultimately it is important to remember that a lot of the recipes I cook and write about were written by wealthy white women who were nostalgic for slavery. Whether there is still value to be found in them is up for debate. I suppose that I must think there is, because I keep cooking them.

When I found out about Michael Twitty's work many years ago I couldn't believe how fortunate we could be in Maryland to have a steward seeking out and compiling the evidence of the origins of our foodways. When his 'Open Letter to Paula Deen' went viral in 2013, Michael Twitty began to take on a role beyond historian, as an arbiter of that history and modern American food culture, with its many questions and contradictions.

Thanks to Twitty's long-awaited book, we have a bit of a rough outline to start the process of acknowledging the many enslaved cooks whose hands and traditions shaped the American food that is inseparable from "our" traditions as a whole in multicultural Maryland.

When I cooked up this fried eggplant from "Maryland's Way," I figured that I would find something to write about Tulip Hill, a historic plantation home in Galesville, Maryland. The house was built around 1755 by Samuel Galloway, a Maryland slave trader who owned several plantations and enslaved at least 87 people on those properties in addition to the "Men, Women, Boys and Girls" whom he sold into slavery.

"...The roots of American soul food began... among the tidal creeks, coastal plain and rolling Piedmont hills in the colonial Chesapeake region between the seventeenth and eighteenth centuries... About 20,000 [enslaved Africans] would be brought to the Catholic colony of Maryland, predominantly from Senegal, Gambia, Ghana and Kongo." – Michael Twitty, The Cooking Gene

In 1948, Tulip Hill was purchased by Hope Andrews and her husband Lewis. In the 1960s, Mrs. Andrews worked closely with Mrs. Frances Kelly to compile "Maryland's Way," perhaps the most beloved of Maryland cookbooks. In 2015, I praised Maryland's Way as a "gargantuan effort" and quoted an article about the five years that the ladies spent testing over 700 recipes for the cookbook.

The credit for the recipe for "Eggplant Fried in Batter", and three others in "Maryland's Way," reads "Tulip Hill, West River, 'Alice's Way.'"

This mononymous accreditation is common in historic recipes that have been appropriated from servants and slaves (when a credit is given at all). You wouldn't know it from reading my blog, but I always make an attempt to tease out these ghosts from census records and any other source I can find. I usually come up empty-handed. This particular recipe, having been contributed by Mrs. Andrews herself, proved to be an exception.

According to an account of "Maryland's Way" in "Outlook By the Bay", Mrs. Kelly and Mrs. Andrews had assistance when they tested the many recipes included in the book:

"They compiled the recipes, but then needed to ensure that they were suitable for modern kitchens. Alice Brown, the cook at Tulip Hill, was tasked with testing them, and they found a willing taste-tester in Mrs. Andrews' teenage nephew Harry Cannon. He vividly remembers Alice preparing all of the recipes as he eagerly watched, waiting to sample the results of her culinary endeavors. He still holds her partially responsible for his lifelong love of cooking and cookbook collecting."

If this article is to be believed, Alice Brown tested and adjusted nearly all of the recipes in "Maryland's Way." These are Maryland recipes that have been duplicated in other books such as the Southern Heritage Cookbooks, reprinted in newspapers, and shared on the internet.

In 1975, the Capital in Annapolis ran a profile of Alice Brown. "We had to cut it all down to teaspoons and tablespoons from pounds," Brown had said of the experience of interpreting the historic recipes. According to the Capital, Brown was the daughter of a tenant farmer from Lothian, Maryland. Although her mother hadn't cooked for a living, she had "loved to prepare fine tasting dishes, and handed down that love to Alice," who inherited her mother's techniques and "a love of fresh farm foods."

A photo accompanying the article shows a copy of the 19th century "Frugal Housekeeper's Kitchen Companion"; a French cookbook; and a copy of "Aunt Priscilla in the Kitchen," a compilation of the racist Baltimore Sun recipe columns of the same name.

The Capital mentions Alice's husband's name as Thomas and that they lived on Mill Swamp Road. Anything further is speculation on my part. An Alice Brown appears in the 1940 census in Anne Arundel county, where she is listed as a Black woman who was a servant for a "private family." I found a 1940 military draft document for a Thomas Brown on Mill Swamp Road, whose wife is listed as Alice Rebecca Brown. Thomas Brown's employment was with the Woodfield Fish & Oyster

Company. There was an Alice Randall born in the early 1900's in Lothian. That family did live on a farm but the patriarch was a blacksmith.

Andrews may have been affecting a historic norm when she attributed the recipe to "Alice" in "Maryland's Way". In doing so, she unwittingly perpetuated the erasure of the contributions of African Americans and of the 'servant class' to Maryland cooking.

In The Cooking Gene, Twitty directed a message to African Americans in particular: "We are not living in the past or for the past. Recognition, credit, acknowledgement, and the learning and transmission of the old ways are all critical. However, we need the best of our food culture as African people in America to move forward to give us opportunity... everything must be put on the table; our food is not just for us, it is a way into an alternative history and a new vision of who we can become."

I think that regardless of ethnicity and genetic origin, everyone has a part in this. In addition to recognizing the legacy of the past in the food we eat today, we can all try to be more aware the ways in which well-meaning people can overlook existing inequality. I like to believe that we can learn from history without glorifying it. ❁

Eggplant Fried in Batter

1 Cup milk
1 medium eggplant
garlic salt
1 egg
1 Cup flour
.5 Teaspoon salt
.125 Teaspoon black pepper
Slice eggplant thin lengthwise. Sprinkle lightly with garlic salt, stack under a weighted plate for   hour. Make a batter by beating the egg and stirring in the flour and remaining seasonings, alternating with the milk. Mix until smooth and bubbly. Drain eggplant and pat dry. Dip each slice in batter and fry until golden brown in hot oil.

Recipe Adapted from "Maryland's Way"

Cinnamon Cake, Zelma T. Cole (a personal essay)

Posted on July 17, 2022

Fairly early in the pandemic, I moved to a new house.

I felt conflicted, leaving the 1880s rowhouse on Howard Street that I'd bought in 2009. But it had some issues that were becoming bothersome. The dining room was cramped and dark, and the kitchen small and awkward, making the increasing Old Line Plate-related press requests to film or photograph me there unfeasible. We'd filmed the 2019 Baltimore Sun bit in my cousin's Medfield kitchen. Plus... I really wanted a porch.

When we went to view the house that would become our new home, we were nervous if it was even ethical to do so, but we couldn't pass up the opportunity. Masked and gloved, we toured a spacious place not far from our own and we made an offer.

Real-estate boringness ensued. Suspenseful for us, dull to read about. Through luck, privilege, a little of my own savvy and diligence (if I do say so myself), and the help of our excellent real estate agent, we somehow ended up moving in May of 2020. We carried half our things on foot.

I soon learned that the model we bought was called a "Daylight Rowhouse." Built to be wider rather than deeper, there was a window in each room. Many of these houses didn't even require skylights. Builders began advertising this style to Baltimore's upwardly mobile around 1915. "Why buy an old house with small dark and ill-ventilated rooms, when a house 20 feet wide, 7 rooms and bath... can be had for the same money?," read one ad in the Sun. Hey! That's how I felt, over a century later! Suffice it to say, we love it here.

Social Distancing turned into a months-long affair and I became more and more depressed. Our good fortune felt wrong – incompatible with everything else going on.

Meanwhile, I researched the house.

I found that our block was built in 1924 by Hopkins graduate

John Dubblede, who took up residence in one of the newly-built houses and proceeded to sell the others throughout the year. In September, Edward G Cole, an insurance agent, bought the house that I now live in.

Twelve years prior, Cole had married Zelma Teal at the Jefferson Street Methodist Episcopal Church on Jefferson & Bond Streets. The church has since been demolished to make way for the Johns Hopkins Hospital complex, but at the time it was just a few blocks away from Zelma's family home at 941 North Broadway.

Our rowhouse might seem like a lateral move for the Coles, by square footage alone. In 1920 they lived at 2713 Guilford Ave. Like me, the Coles moved just a few blocks —in their case from an older Charles Village porch-front house with a bay window. But as I've come to appreciate myself, the "daylight" makes all the difference.

The family must have liked the house as much as I do, because they stayed here for many years, with their daughter Evelyn (born in 1918), and Edward's sister Bessie.

Evelyn went on to be highly involved with the nearby Baltimore Museum of Art as a docent and with the Women's Committee. She was frequently in the Baltimore Sun because of this and other volunteer activities. Her 2001 obituary said that her passion for volunteering began when she was a teenager.

Zelma Cole, on the other hand, lived a more quiet life and appeared in the paper far less frequently. After Edward died in 1953, she remained in the house until selling it in 1967. She moved to 3333 N. Charles Street and died in 1969. She is buried with her husband in Greenmount Cemetery.

At some point, I began to jokingly fantasize about disturbing Zelma's grave so that she would haunt me. I was so lonely and sad. I wanted company in my beautiful new house.

Zelma's biggest brush with the local news was in 1955 when she was quoted in an article about haircuts. "I'll keep my hair short this year because I like it that way," she told the Evening Sun, "but I will admit that during the winter it looks nice just a little bit longer than in the summer. I also think younger people look better with long hair."

What if Zelma came to haunt me and she was completely superficial? What if my only company during awful isolated times was a ghost who only cared about hair and clothes? I contemplated writing a comedic short story but I wasn't feeling hilarious enough to make it happen.

Eventually, I'd found all there was to find about Zelma and the Cole family. Life continued to trudge onward. I took solace in the airy rooms, ample porch, and tidy small yard of my "daylight rowhome."

A year and a day after we moved, I was starting to dig back into the things that I love. I was cooking for the website again, and taking joy in research. I finally got around to mapping the recipes from the 1911 Baltimore Sun recipe contest. I began researching the contributors to the 1936 Lovely Lane Cook Book. I was interested in this one because of all the time I've lived in Charles Village, Remington, and Waverly. I loved seeing all the familiar old houses as I listed the addresses; envisioning the old kitchens.

And then suddenly I couldn't believe my eyes.

"Nut Bread; Cinnamon Cake; Punch; Peach Fritters; Seven Minute Icing"... Mrs. Edward G. Cole.

I reached over and grabbed the arm of my husband, who was sitting beside me on the couch. Zelma Cole's recipes had been in my database this entire time. I'd data-entered them on May 22, 2019, just over one year before we moved.

It never would have occurred to me to search in my own database for Zelma T. Cole. It seemed too improbable. My database, especially the "people" component, is not that big.

But there she was. I pulled up further documents. I looked for other Edward G. Coles. The first results were the familiar censuses I'd viewed months before. Then came the 1940s Draft documents. The other Baltimore 'Edward Coles': unmarried men, without their middle names listed. The Edward at my address: Edward Greenlee Cole. It had to be a match.

It wasn't until the fall that I finally tried one of the recipes, for this quick Cinnamon Cake. It was nice and simple, a good showcase for special cinnamon or other spices. I may make it again. It belongs to my kitchen, after all.

Eventually I tried Zelma's peach fritter recipe. One by one I'll get to them all. I have the rest of my life to do so.

Finding a recipe from a past resident of my own house, already in my database, will always remain one of my most wild and most exhilarating research moments.

I doubt I will experience that kind of coincidence again. But now I have a way to taste the results whenever I want. In doing so, I fulfill my wish from some of my lowest, strangest moments of a desperate time: befriending the ghost of Zelma Teal Cole. ❋

Cinnamon Cake

1 egg
1.5 Cup flour
.75 Cup milk
2 Teaspoon baking powder
.75 Cup sugar
butter the size of a walnut
Mix well and place dough in greased pan, dot with butter, then cover with sugar and cinnamon. Bake fifteen (15) or twenty (20) minutes.

Recipe from "Lovely Lane Cook Book," c. 1936, The Woman's Guild First Methodist Episcopal Church

Jeanette Oettinger's Chocolate Macaroons

From "Festive Maryland Recipes"

One of the first Jewish-American cookbooks, Esther Levy's "Jewish Cookery Book," was published in 1871 in Philadelphia. Like many of its contemporaries, it included household tips for cleaning, repelling vermin, and treating common ailments like asthma, boils, and bad breath. There are many recipes for fish dishes: fried, broiled, potted, in salad. Soup recipes include ox-tail, gumbo, and matzo for Passover. Towards the back of the book, there was a Jewish calendar that listed holidays and dates for the Sabbath.

The preface warned against the idea that "a repast, to be sumptuous, must unavoidably admit of forbidden food." For Levy, cooking well was a matter of piety.

The authors of "Pots, Pans and Pie Plates ¢ How to Use Them," one of the oldest Jewish cookbooks from this state, had a different approach. The book featured lots of regional favorites, including non-kosher fare like Maryland Fried Chicken (with cream gravy), five recipes for crab, and five for oysters. This was Chesapeake country after all.

The 1905 book may have broken from kosher tradition in order to appeal to a broader audience. It's more likely that the recipes simply reflected what the women who compiled the book liked to eat, and that they shared recipes accordingly.

In her 2005 book "Matzoh Ball Gumbo: Culinary Tales of the Jewish South," Marcie Cohen Ferris explored the ways that Jewish people in the South did or did not partake of treyf (nonkosher) foods. "The degree to which southern Jews either embraced local cuisine or preserved Jewish foodways defined their identity in the South." Despite Baltimore being a larger city with potentially better access to kosher foods, the authors of "Pots, Pans and Pie Plates" were manifesting Maryland identity in their cookbook.

Since 1895, the Hebrew Kindergarten and Day Nursery (for

which "Pots, Pans and Pie Plates" was a fundraiser) had provided education to children, especially those of the influx of Russian Jewish immigrants to Baltimore.

A 1900 Baltimore Sun article about the school was headlined "Tots Play at Farming." In addition to the things "taught in all kindergartens," the Hebrew Day Nursery was teaching the children about farming and gardening, housekeeping and cooking. That year, the Sun also described how the kids would observe the Feast of Purim by reciting the story of Queen Esther and enjoying cake and ice cream.

"Pots, Pans and Pie Plates," not only raised funds through cookbook sales, but also through the ads found in the book, for everything from umbrellas, shoes and upholstery to sarsaparilla and corned beef.

After the many breads, pickles, pies, cakes and puddings in the book, there is a section of "Passover Receipts." Mrs. Louis Levin contributed all five recipes, and all involve matzo meal.

Local newspapers occasionally reported on Passover, with a special curiosity for matzo. In March 1893, the Frederick News Post wrote that "a great many large bake shops in Baltimore have been engaged since the first of the year in turning out nothing but unleavened bread... A matzath [sic] cake is round, about four inches in diameter, slightly browned and having tiny air hole protuberances on its surface. They have a rather pleasant taste not unlike that of crackers, and make an excellent substitute for bread..."

Another popular Passover treat is macaroons, which contain no flour or leavening. "Pots, Pans and Pie Plates" contained several recipes for them. Mrs. Jeanette Oettinger (1841-1947) provided the one adapted here, containing chocolate and cloves. Oettinger and her husband Frank (1825-1911) immigrated from Germany, and became prominent philanthropists in Baltimore, involved with a network of charities aiming to uplift and acclimate impoverished and/or recently immigrated Jews at the turn of the 20th century. The umbrella organization, The Federated Jewish Charities, became part of "The Associated: Jewish Federation of Baltimore," which is still active today.

"Pots, Pans and Pie Plates" served its religious ends not through strict adherence to traditional dietary laws, but through its charitable cause. According to the Talmud, charity, or tzedakah, "is equal to all the other commandments combined." ❋

Macaroons (Chocolate)

Whites of 6 eggs
    pound of confectioners' sugar
1 cake of Bakers' chocolate
    ounce of cinnamon
    teaspoonful of ground cloves
Add the sugar gradually to the whites, first beaten to a stiff froth. Then add the grated chocolate, with which the spices have been thoroughly mixed. Drop into pans and bake in moderate oven.

Recipe from "Pots, Pans and Pie Plates," 1905, The Hebrew Day Nursery

Chocolate Macaroons

Jeannette and Henry Oettinger

1858-1908

September Nineteenth

Jewish Museum of Maryland

Ginger Pound Cakes, McCormick Manual of Cookery c. 1912

Posted on December 21, 2023

"Some one has said that every big man has a hobby," according to an article in the Baltimore Sun in 1915. "Willoughby M. McCormick is no exception to the rule... He has two hobbies that go together. One is food quality in connection with food purity, and the other is domestic science, or the science of cookery. Under his direction [McCormick Spice Company] has published a splendid manual of Cookery."

McCormick's Manual of Cookery was first published in the early 1910s. By 1914, it was retitled "Bee Brand Manual of Cookery: The Blue Book of The Culinary Art."

The 1915 article in the Baltimore Sun boasted that the manual was "full of recipes from the best cooks of Maryland and the Virginias, in which dishes are preserved from the Colonial period—dishes which gave the South the gastronomic championship of the world." Once again, "Colonial" was used as a euphemism for antebellum times. Even the McCormick cookery book capitalized on a romanticized vision of Southern hospitality.

McCormick shared some interesting opinions in the article. He didn't think the Pure Foods law went far enough. His brand, he said, used more vanilla than legally required in their extract. He liked for consumers to visit his plant downtown to get firsthand confidence in his products. "Each consumer is our personal customer," he said. He felt that "purity and quality and preparation of food are at the bottom of the misery or happiness of a nation of people."

McCormick believed that men should teach their daughters about finance. "They do that nicely, over in France," he said. "In this country women spend money as if it were nothing." As an example, he mentioned women who bought artificial vanilla extract "from old women and cripples who peddle from door to door." The Sun entitled this section of the article "Spending Money Foolishly."

The article's writer visited that McCormick plant and was enchanted. "A journey through the McCormick house would pay anyone who desired swift transportation from the humdrum modern business life to the atmosphere of the Far East, with its romance and fragrances," they wrote, describing the plant as "the Kingdom of the Sounds of Odors, where very delight wafted to the nostrils is a song or a poem."

The Bee Brand Manual of Cookery was marketed in at least a few newspapers around the country, and in the Boston Cooking School magazine. The ads within the Bee Brand Manual itself show what a wide variety of products once bore the McCormick name, from glue to insect poison to tea to tapioca.

The book opens with soup, starting with "Almond Soup," made from almonds, celery, milk, stock, onions, and of course 1 teaspoon Bee Brand Whole White Peppers. A "Things Worth Knowing" section contains tips for removing stains and treating burns, mad dog and snake bites. Beneath a recommended procedure for reviving a person who has fainted, the book gives "Tests of Death:"

"Hold mirror to mouth. If living, moisture will gather. Push pin into flesh. If dead, the hole will remain, if alive it will close up."

Although the different editions of the McCormick and Bee Brand Manuals have most of the same recipes, there were some minor changes. I made a Ginger Pound Cake recipe that appeared in the c. 1912 McCormick's Manual of Cookery but was removed from later editions, probably to make room for other spices. The McCormick's manual has a dozen recipes centered around ginger. The Bee Brand book has half that.

The paper that most cookbooks were printed on in the early 20th century tends to be fairly frail. As such, there are not too many copies of the Bee Brand Manual in libraries or for sale. I took it upon myself to scan mine for the Internet Archive. I figured the more people who know a reliable "test of death," the better. It is, after all, a thing worth knowing. ❁

Ginger Pound Cakes

.75 Cup butter
1 Cup sugar
1 Cup molasses
3 Cups flour
.5 Teaspoon baking soda
1 Cup milk
2 eggs
1 Teaspoon Bee Brand ground cloves
1 Teaspoon Bee Brand ground cinnamon
1 Tablespoon Bee Brand ground ginger
Beat butter and sugar till creamy, then add eggs well
beaten, molasses, flour, soda dissolved in milk, and
spices. Turn into buttered and floured cake tin and bake
in moderate oven for one hour.

Recipe from McCormick's Manual of Cookery. c. 1912.

BEE BRAND

MANUAL
OF
COOKERY

THE BLUE BOOK
OF
THE CULINARY ART

REG. U. S.

REGISTERED TRADE MARK

PAT. OFF

FOR CHILD'S EDITION—
SEE PAGES 186 TO 196

Horse's Collar, John A. Weaver

Posted on February 16, 2024

"Tom Smith liked clothes."

The Afro-American covered every detail of Thomas R. Smith's 1938 funeral. Five women wept. "Two were relatives." United States Senator George Radcliffe spoke at the service, which was held on the lawn of Smith's home at 6621 Reisterstown Road. Inside the house, Tom's body was dressed in striped trousers; a satin, striped black ascot; and a black coat with a gardenia in the buttonhole. In his closet, he left sixteen pairs of white shoes, silk shirts and boxers, and "innumerable suits of all kinds, colors and materials."

On the lawn of Smith's home, across from where Reisterstown Plaza now sits, mourners interacted with his herd of goats, who demanded to have their heads scratched. One goat chewed on a political poster announcing a candidate for governor.

This is not about Tom Smith; not really. But I can't write about John Weaver, who tended bar at Smith's Hotel for twenty-six years and called his boss "Chief," without writing about Smith himself.

How could I not include the fact that Smith, according to the Afro-American "maintained his dominion by aid of an elaborate set-up which prevented any illegal business being conducted without his knowledge or consent," or that he influenced Baltimore's Black citizens to vote Democrat in a time when that was unheard of?

I can't leave out the eleven homes Smith left behind, the stocks he owned in white hotels including the Southern, and a reported fortune in jewelry. One ring had been pawned to him by the mother of Wallis Warfield, Duchess of Windsor. According to the Afro-American, "It was a chief sport of his to exhibit these precious stones to feminine friends and see the glitter in their eyes. But they seldom, if ever, got beyond merely trying on one of the lovely rings. Yet he allowed a relative, a mere boy, to wear for months a diamond ring worth thousands." (Note: A thousand dollars in 1938 is equivalent to almost $22,000 today.)

For years, the Afro ran a news feature entitled "Smith's Hotel," listing the people staying each week in its 26 rooms.

The hotel stood at 437 Druid Hill Avenue. The bar was a place for politicians, movers-and-shakers, and would-be beneficiaries of Smith's famous generosity.

The bar occupied most of the hotel's first floor. The elaborate hand-carved bartop had cost a pretty penny. Before the hotel, Smith had run a saloon on Jasper Street from 1900-1912, raising the significant funds he needed to open his next venture.

Much less is known about John Avery Weaver, the man behind the bar. He was born in Baltimore in 1886 to Walter T. Weaver and Sarah (maiden name Falland.) In the early 1900s, he began bartending in Baltimore's exclusive clubs before leaving for Atlantic City, where he worked behind the bars of several hotels. By the time he returned to Baltimore to work for Smith, he'd had experience serving the fickle and particular tastes of famous and powerful people. He lived as 1212 Druid Hill Avenue and later, on Pitcher Street.

In 1938, the Afro ran a series of columns containing drink recipes from Weaver, "one of the leading bartenders of the East." He provided formulas for Fish House Punch, Manhattan Cocktail, Whiskey Smash, Sloe Gin Fizz, and other cocktails. I noticed that his recipe for Horse's Collar, a drink that sometimes contains Brandy, was a non-alcoholic version using bitters and the rind of an entire lemon.

I am sure that one of "America's Best Mixologists" had some flamboyant way of cutting said lemon peel, which I could not hope to achieve. My lackluster presentation aside, with three healthy dashes of bitters, Weaver's recipe sits well among the growing number of alcohol alternatives being made behind bars today.

Weaver died in 1961 after a two-year stay in Crownsville State Hospital. His career as a Bartender is enshrined under "occupation" on his death certificate, a memento of a time when that profession garnered prestige to rival the famed chefs and caterers.

Smith's hotel never quite found its footing after the death of its owner. Smith's brother Wallace ran the hotel until he was killed in a mugging in 1939. In 1944, the hotel was sold to a white owner. In 1957, the building was razed for a parking lot.

Later, newspapers would reminisce about the hotel and its heyday. A photo showing the life-sized photograph of Joe Gans in the hotel lobby might appear in these articles, next to a picture of the hotel's exterior festooned with patriotic decor. Another photograph frequently reprinted was of the bar, with Weaver standing confidently amongst hundreds of bottles, in a crisp white suit, one elbow leaned against the bar.

Weaver returned for the hotel's re-opening in 1940, then known as the "Memory Bar at Smith's Hotel." The name would prove all too apt. With both Tom and Wallace Smith gone, the hotel could not regain its momentum and would soon close again.

In 2023, author Toni-Tipton Martin released a book called "Juke Joints, Jazz Clubs, and Juice: A Cocktail Recipe Book: Cocktails from Two Centuries of African American Cookbooks." As with her previous books, The Jemima Code and Jubilee, Tipton-Martin is working to rectify the erasure of the Black stories in culinary history. Tom Smith and John Weaver attracted patrons across the color barrier in a segregated city. While Smith managed business and wielded political influence, Weaver proudly practiced his craft, making sure that imbibers and teetotalers alike were welcomed into the dazzling world built from the ground up by Tom Smith. ❀

Horse's Collar

1 large block ice
1 lemon rind
3 dashes Angostura bitters
ginger ale

Use large glass. Place 1 large block ice, the rind of a whole lemon, 3 dashes Angostura Bitters. Fill glass with ginger ale and serve with straw.

Recipe from the Afro-American, September 30th, 1939

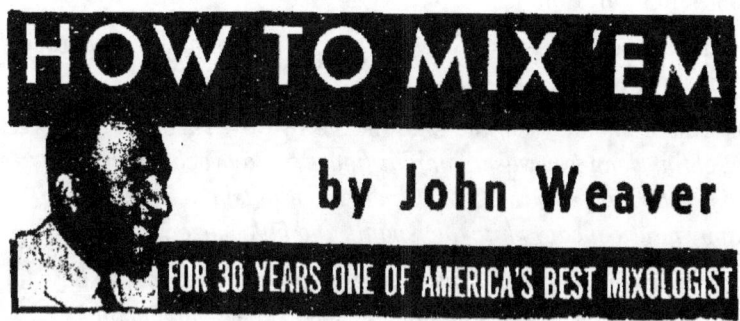

HOW TO MIX 'EM
by John Weaver
FOR 30 YEARS ONE OF AMERICA'S BEST MIXOLOGIST

Have you tried the Remsen Cooler? If you haven't, then, you've been missing something. It's inexpensive, extremely palatable and easy to concoct. Here's how:

REMSEN COOLER

Use large glass. Large Lump ice, rind of whole lemon; 1 drink gin or scotch. Fill glass with plain soda. — Serve.

Frank Hennessy's "Chicken-Boh-B-Q"

Posted on April 21, 2017

Frank Hennessy never passed up a chance to promote National Beer. It was his job to do so for 18 years (1957 to 1975), and he approached the job with legendary gusto.

Advertising executive John Schneider III (1918-2009) has been credited with "making Boh synonymous with Baltimore." He may also share part of the credit for making the name "Frank Hennessy" synonymous with Boh. It was Schneider who put Hennessy aboard a skipjack named "Chester Peake" and sent him "to every corner of Tidewater Maryland" as the "Roving Ambassador of the Chesapeake Bay."

The sail of the 1915 skipjack was embroidered with the face of the iconic "Mr. Boh."

When Hennessy passed away in 2000, the Sun had many stories to share:

"Dubbed 'Commodore of the Chesapeake' by Gov. Theodore Roosevelt McKeldin, Hennessy was a familiar figure to Bay yachtsman as he cruised the Bay from the C & D Canal to Smith Island, dressed in a snappy nautical cap, white duck pants and blue blazer.

'During the summer months we'll be cruising the Chesapeake Bay, attending races, regattas and other special events, hoping that Chester Peake will serve as a graceful symbol of the wonderful Land of Pleasant Living,' [Hennessy] told The Sun.

Hennessy, an excellent outdoors cook who gained honors as the Male Barbecuing Champion at the national chicken grill-off in Selbyville, Del., was the creator of the Chesapeake BAYke.

'We have our wonderful crab feasts, oyster and bull roasts but there's no identifying name like New England clambake or Hawaiian luau, and my wife and I got to thinking about a Chesapeake BAYke,' he told The Sun in an interview.

Firing up his gigantic Weber Big Smokey grill, Hennessy and his wife, Rita, whom he married in 1938, used such strictly local Maryland ingredients as rockfish, clams, oysters, blue crabs, corn and broiler chicken to create the feast.

Hennessy, who was born in St. Louis and reared in Memphis, always claimed one of his grilling secrets was using Arkansas swamp hickory chips." – True Chesapeake Character, Frederick N. Rasmussen, Baltimore Sun, 2000

The concept of the somewhat-awkwardly-named Chesapeake BAYke provided Hennessy with more opportunities to promote Natty Boh in local newspapers.

He copyrighted the term in 1964.

In 1960, Hennessy took home the prize in the Barbecue division of the Delmarva Poultry Industry's National Chicken Cooking Contest. His recipe for a broiled and basted chicken features a not-so-secret addition. You guessed it.

I remember my own introduction to Boh. After watching a friend's band at the Ottobar in the late 90s, we migrated to the bar upstairs. Someone asked what beer was the cheapest. "Natty Boh-boh!" was a friend's lyrical reply. At a buck fifty, no one needed any further rationale for drinking National Bohemian.

A lot of Baltimoreans still carry the banner of Natty Boh from bars to backyard barbecues, despite the fact that the beer is now brewed in North Carolina and Georgia. It no longer costs a buck fifty, but neither does anything else. Nor are you likely to hear about raconteurs cruising the bay for the sole purpose of glorifying a beer. The unchanging label of Natty Boh remains a reminder of a time when Baltimore was a little bit cheaper and a little bit weirder. ❊

Chicken-Boh-B-Q

1/4 cup melted butter
2 tablespoons lemon juice
1/2 teaspoon orange extract
1/4 teaspoon tapasco
1 teaspoon monosodium glutamate
1 teaspoon salt
1/4 teaspoon fresh ground pepper
1 tablespoon dark black molasses
1 tablespoon brown sugar
1 teaspoon grated orange rind

Heat sauce over charcoal fire while waiting for flames to die down. A few moist hickory chips added to the charcoal will give a hickory-smoked flavor.

Coat broiler halves with sauce before placing on grill. Continue basting while cooking. Broiler halves should cook slowly so they will be tender and juicy on the inside, golden brown on the outside. Time will vary between 45 minutes and 1 1/2 hours depending on heat from coals and size of broiler.

When chicken is done, "glaze" by quickly pouring beer over both sides of each half before removing from grill.

If more of a "bite" is desired add more tabasco.

Recipe adapted from.National Chicken Cooking Contest Cookbook, 1971, Delmarva Poultry Industry. Inc.

23rd ANNUAL

NATIONAL CHICKEN COOKING CONTEST RECIPES

1ST PRIZE

$1.00

1971

Selected Bibliography

The Woman's Guild. Lovely Lane Cook Book. First Methodist Episcopal Church. 1936.

Miss Leida A. Willis [Lida Ames Willis]. Rumford Cook Book. Rumford Chemical Works. Providence, RI. 1895.

The Afro-American Newspapers.

Annapolis Capital Gazette; The Baltimore Afro-American; Baltimore Sun/ Evening Sun; Baltimore City Paper; Chicago Weekly Post; The Cumberland News;

Baltimore Gas & Electric Company. Maryland Classics. Baltimore Gas & Electric Company. 1985.

The Baltimore Sun (Evening).

Bethel A.M.E. Church. Bethel Cookbook. Baltimore, MD. 1979.

The Art of Confectionery: With Various Methods of Preserving Fruits and Fruit Juices United States, J. E. Tilton, 1865.

Averill, E. W.. Alum in baking powder. United States, n.p, 1927.

Bader, Bonnie. Curious About Ice Cream. United States, Penguin Young Readers Group, 2017.

Barrett, Heather. Our History, Our Heritage, 31 Mar. 2021.

Beirne, Francis F.. The Amiable Baltimoreans. United States, Johns Hopkins University Press, 1984.

Bernard, Shane K.. Tabasco, an Illustrated History: The Story of the McIlhenny Family of Avery Island, 1868-2007. United States, McIlhenny Company, 2007.

Blum, Deborah. The Poison Squad: One Chemist's Single-Minded Crusade for Food Safety at the Turn of the Twentieth Century. United States, Penguin Publishing Group, 2019.

Blume, Bruce & Lambright, Katie & Tomko, Sara. Snobaltimore. Baltimore Snoball Collective, Baltimore, 2011.

Brown, Dona. Inventing New England: Regional Tourism in the Nineteenth Century. United States, Smithsonian, 2014.

Buckeye Cookery and Practical Housekeeping. United States, Buckeye Publishing Company, 1877.

Centenary United Methodist. Our Daily Bread. 1961, 1982.

Civitello, Linda. Baking Powder Wars: The Cutthroat Food Fight that Revolutionized Cooking. United States, University of Illinois Press, 2017.

Croly, Jane Cunningham. Jennie June's American Cookery Book. United States, Excelsior, 1878.

Delmarva Poultry Industry. Inc.. 1971 National Chicken Cooking Contest Cookbook. 1971.

Delmarva Poultry Industry. Prize Winning Del-Mar-Va-Lous Chicken Recipes 1949 & 1950. Delmarva Chicken Festival, Inc.. Dover, DE. 1950.

The Dispenser's Formulary: Or, Soda Water Guide. United States, D.O. Haynes & Company, 1915.

E. [Elizabeth Isabella] Purviance recipe book, undated , in the Purviance family papers collection, David M. Rubenstein Rare Book & Manuscript Library, Duke University.

The Episcopal Church Women of St. Paul's Parish. Queen Anne Goes to the Kitchen (1993). Tidewater Publishers. 1993.

Epworth League of Still Pond Methodist Episcopal Church. The Eastern Shore Cook Book. Still Pond, MD. 1919.

Filippini, Alessandro. The Delmonico Cook Book. N.p., Applewood Books, 2008.

Freedman, Paul. Ten Restaurants That Changed America. United States, Liveright, 2016.

Frick family papers, MS 2703. H. Furlong Baldwin Library.

Fulton, Chandos. A Brown Stone Front: A Story of New York and Saratoga. N.p., Research Publications, 1873.

Gaige, Crosby. New York World's Fair Cook Book: The American Kitchen. United States, Doubleday, Doran, Incorporated, 1939.

Mrs. J. H. Giese. The Practical Cook Book. Hanzche & Company. Batimore. 1888.

Mrs. Charles H. Gibson. Mrs. Charles H. Gibson's Maryland And Virginia Cookbook. John Murphy & Co.. Baltimore. 1894.

Gaskins, Ruth L.. A Good Heart and a Light Hand. United States, Fund for Alexandria, Virginia, 1968.

Glasse, Hannah. The Art of Cookery Made Plain and Easy. United Kingdom, W. Strahan [and 25 others], 1784.

H. Franklyn Hall. 300 Ways to Cook and Serve Shell Fish. Christian Banner Print. Philadelphia, PA. 1901.

The Hammond-Harwood House Association. Maryland's Way. The Hammond-Harwood House Association. 1966.

Harris, Evelyn. The Barter Lady: A Woman Farmer Sees it Through. United States, Doubleday, Doran, Incorporated, 1934.

Hayward, Mary Ellen, and Belfoure, Charles. The Baltimore Rowhouse. United States, Princeton Architectural Press, 2012.

Hess, Karen, and Randolph, Mary. The Virginia House-wife. United States, University of South Carolina Press, 1984.

Horsey, Patricia Joan O.. Legendary Locals of Kent County. United States, Arcadia Publishing Incorporated, 2015.

Mrs. Benjamin Chew Howard. Fifty Years in a Maryland Kitchen. J. B. Lippincott Co. 1873.

Ladies Aid Society of the Church of the Holy Comforter. The Favorite Receipt Book and Business Directory. Trade Press. 1884.

Ladies Aid Society of the Methodist Episcopal Church, North East. Maryland Recipes Tried and True. Elkton Appeal Press. Elkton, MD. 1901.

Ladies of St. Paul Lutheran Church, Uniontown Maryland. Choice Maryland Cookery. Printed at the Caroll Record Office. 1902.

Ladies of the Presbyterian Church, Chesapeake City. Tested Maryland Recipes. Cecil Whig Publishing. Elkton, MD. 1900.

Elizabeth Ellicott Lea. Domestic cookery, useful receipts, and hints to young housekeepers. 2004.

Littell's Living Age. United States, T. H. Carter & Company, 1844.

Lockwood, Charles, et al. Bricks & Brownstone: The New York Row House. Italy, Rizzoli, 2019.

Lohman, Sarah. Eight Flavors: The Untold Story of American Cuisine. United States, Simon & Schuster, 2016.

Maryland, a Guide to the Old Line State,. N.p., Best Books on, 1940.

Maryland Home Economics Association. Maryland Cooking. 1948.

May, Robert. The Accomplisht Cook. N.p., Outlook Verlag, 2020.

Michener, James A.. Chesapeake: A Novel. United States, Random House Publishing Group, 2013.

Miller, Adrian. Soul Food: The Surprising Story of an American Cuisine, One Plate at a Time. United States, University of North Carolina Press, 2013.

Murrey, Thomas Jefferson. Cookery with a Chafing Dish. United States, F.A. Stokes Company, 1891.

Niernsee, Emily. Emily [Bradenbaugh] Niernsee's cookbook (1861). MS 2457. H Furlong Baldwin Library

Peril, Lynn. College Girls: Bluestockings, Sex Kittens, and Co-Eds, Then and Now. W. W. Norton & Company, 2006. Bill Phillips. What Is Cooking On Party Line. Broad Creek Printing. 1983.

The Practice of Cookery and Pastry: Adapted to the Business of Every Day Life. United Kingdom, W. Forrester, 1849.

Mary Randolph. The Virginia Housewife Or, Methodical Cook. Dover Publications, Inc.. New York. 1824.

Ranhofer, Charles. The Epicurean. United States, R. Ranhofer, 1916.

Reber, Patricia Bixler. Researching Food History, http://researchingfoodhistory.blogspot. com/.

Rigby, Fred, and Rigby, Will O.. Rigby's Reliable Candy Teacher. United States, Rigby Publishing Company, 1920.

Roberts, Mabel. Cookbooks n. d., MS 2755. H. Furlong Baldwin Library

Roberts, Winthrop A.. The Crab Industry of Maryland. United States, U.S. Government Printing Office, 1905.

Mrs. Virginia Roeder. Fun With Sea Food. The Baltimore Evening Sun. 1960.

Schaaf, Elizabeth M., and Hildebrand, David K.. Musical Maryland: A History of Song and Performance from the Colonial Period to the Age of Radio. Johns Hopkins University Press, 2017.

Senior Class of Western High School. Soul Food Cookbook. 1971.

Sherwood, John. Maryland's Vanishing Lives. United Kingdom, Johns Hopkins University Press, 1995.

John Shields. Chesapeake Bay Cooking with John Shields. Broadway Books. New York, NY. 1998.

Shields, David S.. Southern Provisions: The Creation and Revival of a Cuisine. United Kingdom, University of Chicago Press, 2015.

Slackwater Archive, St. Mary's College of Maryland

Slow Food USA

Smith, John. The Journals of Captain John Smith: A Jamestown Biography. United States, National Geographic Society, 2007.

Southern Heritage Cookbook Library. All Pork (Southern Heritage). Oxmoor House. Birmingham, AL. 1984.

Southern Heritage Cookbook Library. Family Gatherings (Southern Heritage). Oxmoor House. Birmingham, AL. 1984.

Southern Heritage Cookbook Library. Pies & Pastry (Southern Heritage). Oxmoor House. Birmingham, AL. 1984.

Southern Heritage Cookbook Library. Plain & Fancy Poultry (Southern Heritage). Oxmoor House. Birmingham, AL. 1983. Frederick Philip Stieff. Eat, Drink & Be Merry In Maryland. Johns Hopkins University Press. Baltimore, MD. 1998.

Mrs. E. J. Strasburg. Maryland Cook Book. Fleet, McGinley & Co. Baltimore. 1902.

Tawes Nursing Home. Grannie's Goodies from Somerset County. 1970.

Tipton-Martin, Toni. The Jemima Code: Two Centuries of African American Cookbooks. United States, University of Texas Press, 2015.

The Truth about Baking Powders. United States, Calumet Baking Powder Company, 1928.

Twitty, Michael W.. The Cooking Gene: A Journey Through African American Culinary History in the Old South. United States, HarperCollins, 2018.

Twitty, Michael. Fighting Old Nep: Foodways of Enslaved Afro-Marylanders, 1634-1864. United States, n.p, 2006.

unknown. Cookbook of Maryland and Virginia Recipes [manuscript]. American Antiquarian Society Library. c 1910.

Want to Start a Revolution? Radical Women in the Black Freedom Struggle. United Kingdom, NYU Press, 2009.

Whitaker, Jan. Restaurant-Ing through History, https://restaurant-ingthroughhistory.com.

White, Joyce. A Taste of History, https://atasteofhistory.net/.

WHITE, Andrew. A Briefe Relation of the Voyage Vnto Maryland. N.p., n.p, 1899.

Williams-Forson, Psyche A.. Building Houses Out of Chicken Legs: Black Women, Food, and Power. United States, University of North Carolina Press, 2006.

Wilson, Bee. "Social Media and the Great Recipe Explosion: Does More Mean Better? | Food | The Guardian." The Guardian, The Guardian, 18 June 2017.

Women's Club Of Melwood District. The Melwood Cook Book. Rosaryville, MD. 1920.
The Food Timeline; The Frederick News Post; Los Angeles Times; The New York Times;
The Staunton Spectator; Wikipedia

Other Old Line Plate titles

Festive Maryland Recipes:
Holiday Traditions from the Old Line State

With recipes gathered from libraries, manuscripts, and the Old Line Plate collection of over 300 regional cookbooks, this expedition through history and geography weaves together the stories of people from around the world who have made a home in Maryland.

Indulge in a Kinkling on Fat Tuesday; celebrate Passover and Easter in East Baltimore; taste cookies from the oldest Maryland cookbook; be the first to visit neighbors on New Year's Day in St. Mary's County; engage in Christmas mayhem and blame the eggnog; find out why the Frostburg post office smells like saffron in December; stuff your Thanksgiving turkey with oysters from the Eastern Shore, and please, don't forget the sauerkraut!

Holidays in the Old Line State have taken many forms, but there is usually something good on the table, drawing family and friends together. Come make a plate.

Old Line Plate
Stories &Recipes from Maryland

This book collects over 40 Old Line Plate posts, with lavish illustrations and a bibliography of Maryland cookbooks.

available on oldlineplate.com